CHILD MALTREATMENT
AND OPTIMAL CAREGIVING
IN SOCIAL CONTEXTS

MICHIGAN STATE UNIVERSITY SERIES
ON CHILDREN, YOUTH, AND FAMILIES
VOLUME I
GARLAND REFERENCE LIBRARY OF SOCIAL SCIENCE
VOLUME 1007

Michigan State University Series on Children, Youth, and Families

Joanne G. Keith, John Paul McKinney, *Senior Editors*
Lawrence B. Schiamberg, *MSU Series Editor*

CHILD MALTREATMENT
AND OPTIMAL CAREGIVING
IN SOCIAL CONTEXTS
by Diana Baumrind

CHILD MALTREATMENT AND OPTIMAL CAREGIVING IN SOCIAL CONTEXTS

DIANA BAUMRIND

GARLAND PUBLISHING, INC.
NEW YORK AND LONDON
1995

Library of Congress Cataloging-in-Publication Data

Baumrind, Diana, 1927–
    Child maltreatment and optimal caregiving in social contexts /
by Diana Baumrind.
        p.   cm. — (Michigan State University series on children, youth,
and families ; v. 1)   (Garland reference library of social science ; v. 1007)
        Includes bibliographical references and index.
        ISBN 0-8153-1918-5 (alk. paper)
        1. Child abuse—United States.   2. Abusive parents—United States.
I. Title.   II. Series.   III. Series: Garland reference library of social science ;
v. 1007.
HV6626.52.B38   1995
362.7'61'0973—dc20   95–17454
                                                                                            CIP

Printed on acid-free, 250-year-life paper
Manufactured in the United States of America

Contents

Outreach Scholarship for Children, Youth, and Families

Richard M. Lerner

The publication of Diana Baumrind's erudite and socially significant volume, *Child Maltreatment and Optimal Caregiving in Social Contexts*, marks the inauguration of the Michigan State University Series on Children, Youth, and Families. Baumrind's insightful and incisive writing, accompanied by the important and stimulating ideas found in the foreword by Paul H. Mussen and in the commentaries by Jacquelyne Faye Jackson and L. Annette Abrams, exemplify the integration of cutting-edge scholarship about America's diverse children, families, and communities with issues pertinent to both social policy and program design, delivery, and evaluation.

As such, Baumrind's volume represents a superb illustration of the scholarly goals of the Institute for Children, Youth, and Families (ICYF). It also constitutes an excellent example of how outreach scholarship can engage policy and intervention programming issues. Moreover, it also stands as impressive evidence that the MSU series, launched by ICYF through the professional commitment, dedication, and intellectual leadership of Professors Lawrence B. Schiamberg, Joanne G. Keith, and John Paul McKinney, and through the visionary support of Marie Ellen Larcada of Garland Publishing, is a scholarly activity that can productively engage the best minds in the research, policy, and programming communities in integrative efforts to use scholarship to enhance the life chances of America's diverse children, youth, and families. Baumrind's volume and the MSU series that it has launched help substantiate the importance and feasibility of the mission ICYF is pursuing.

The ICYF derives its mission from the MSU vision of the nature of a land-grant institution (Lerner & Miller, 1993; Lerner et al., 1994; Miller & Lerner, 1994). This vision is shaped by the model of human development prototypically associated with these institutions' colleges of home economics (or, as they are often now termed, colleges of human ecology, human development, or family science). Using developmental systems thinking as a conceptual frame, the Institute for Children, Youth, and Families seeks to develop initiatives that not only integrate theoretical and empirical approaches to human development with the features of the social, institutional, cultural and historical contexts within which people live, but also create connections between such scholarship and the "worlds" of social policy and of program design, delivery, and evaluation.

The Michigan State University Series on Children, Youth, and Families exemplifies the type of outreach scholarship activity pursued at the ICYF. The series seeks to publish reference and professional works—including book-length monographs and edited volumes—which appeal to a wide audience in communities as well as in universities: Scholars, practitioners, program professionals, service deliverers, child and family advocates, business leaders, policymakers, and youth and family members are all potential parts of the audience that may be interested in the range of books that we envision will appear in the MSU series. Indeed, and as I believe is superbly illustrated by Diana Baumrind's volume, the series will have this broad appeal because of its superordinate themes of the integration of research and outreach and thus of cooperative, collaborative relationships between academe and communities.

Universities, and the scholars who work within them, are at an important crossroads in the history of American higher education (Boyer, 1990, 1994; Lerner, Terry, McKinney, & Abrams, 1994). Community, business, and governmental bodies, all stakeholders in the funding and functioning of universities, are increasingly and more persistently demanding that institutions of higher education use their scholarly resources to address issues of concern to the stakeholders, and to do so in terms that the stakeholders see as valid and valuable (Votruba, 1992). Simply, then, the communities of America are seeking a greater commitment to outreach on the part of their universities. As America's premier land-grant university, Michigan State University is committed to weaving outreach throughout the fabric of the university (Provost's Committee on University Outreach, 1993).

The volume by Diana Baumrind is an ideal way to launch this program. We at ICYF are extremely proud and grateful to have this significant book by one of our nation's most distinguished scholars published as the inaugural contribution to the MSU series.

REFERENCES

Boyer, E. L. (1990). *Scholarship reconsidered: Priorities of the professoriate.* Princeton, NJ: The Carnegie Foundation for the Advancement of Teaching.

Boyer, E. L. (1994, March 9). Creating the new American college [Point of View column]. *The Chronicle of Higher Education* (p. A48).

Lerner, R. M., & Miller, J. R. (1993). Integrating human development research and intervention for America's children: The Michigan State University model. *Journal of Applied Developmental Psychology, 14,* 347–364.

Lerner, R. M., Miller, J. R., Knott, J. H., Corey, K. E., Bynum, T. S., Hoopfer, L. C., McKinney, M. H., Abrams, L. A., Hula, R. C., & Terry, P. A. (1994). Integrating scholarship and outreach in human development research, policy, and service: A developmental contextual perspective. In D. L. Featherman, R. M. Lerner, & M. Perlmutter (Eds.), *Life-span development and behavior, 12* (pp. 249–273). Hillsdale, NJ: Erlbaum.

Lerner, R. M., Terry, P. A., McKinney, M. H., & Abrams, L. A. (1994). Addressing child poverty within the context of a community-collaborative university: Comments on Fabes, Martin, and Smith (1994) and McLoyd (1994). *Family and Consumer Sciences Research Journal, 23,* 67–75.

Miller, J. R., & Lerner, R. M. (1994). Integrating research and outreach: Developmental contextualism and the human ecological perspective. *Home Economics Forum, 7,* 21–28.

Provost's Committee on University Outreach. (1993). *University outreach at Michigan State University: Extending knowledge to serve society: A report by the Provost's Committee on University Outreach.* Michigan State University.

Votruba, J. C. (1992). Promoting the extension of knowledge in service to society. *Metropolitan Universities, 3* (3), 72–80.

Paul H. Mussen

Most social scientists are humane, concerned citizens who sincerely wish that their scholarly and research activities would prove useful in promoting human welfare and alleviating contemporary social horrors such as civil wars, delinquency, violence, ethnic prejudice, and child maltreatment, the issue addressed in the present volume. Yet ordinarily these scientists focus their efforts on basic ("pure") research, conceptualization, and the formulation of theory; potential applications of the scientific findings to policymaking and to the solution of social problems are not usually spelled out.

Fortunately this picture has changed recently, especially since 1980. Some leading social scientists (for example, Edward Zigler, Alberta Seigel, Harold Stevenson, Aletha Huston) have authored or edited books and papers on social problems, including poverty, homelessness, adolescent pregnancy, teenage suicide, and substance abuse. These insightful, provocative publications generally advocate interventions (usually of a psychological nature), new social policies, and/or changes in institutional practices that would, if actualized, have important, wide-ranging, beneficial effects. Yet the scientific information underlying the recommendations, the relationships between systematic studies and their implications for practice, are seldom delineated. Although epidemiological, statistical, and correlational studies may be cited, they are rarely described or evaluated in detail. The present brief volume represents a notable exception to these generalizations. The major portion, Baumrind's essay, is a compelling demonstration of how comprehensive, in-depth investigation and critical evaluation of a vast number of pertinent research and theoretical works can lead directly to specific recommendations for policymakers and for revisions in procedures of welfare agencies.

Following Baumrind's pioneering research, it is generally acknowledged that in normal families a successful balance of parental responsiveness (warmth, reciprocity, and attachment) and demandingness (firm control, monitoring, positive and negative reinforcement) is good for children, promoting their welfare, competence, and social and emotional adjustment. To achieve such a balance, which is characteristic of the "authoritative" pattern of childrearing, caregivers must monitor and supervise their own behavior and their children's behavior carefully and continuously. This, in turn, requires a substantial investment of time, energy, and resources. Favorable childrearing practices are not ordinarily present in abusive homes, characterized by neglect and aversive treatment of children.

What accounts for this situation? Baumrind's critical, closely reasoned analysis of the conditions in families at high risk for child maltreatment, based on a meticulous review of relevant studies, led her to conclude that "the primary causes and cures of child maltreatment [are] attributable primarily to social-structural rather than to psychological factors." Vivid, thought-provoking sections of the essay depict in concrete terms the life conditions and life quality of families most at risk for child maltreatment—families in poverty ("the environmental condition most strongly associated with child abuse" [p. 30]), single parents, marital discord and divorce, adoption and foster care, the presence of difficult children—the social and economic pressures and constraints they encounter, and the hardships of their struggle for survival. In emphasizing the impact of social and social-structural variables, Baumrind's analyses and ideas reflect the current fruitful trend of contextualism in the social sciences, illustrated in the writings of Richard Lerner, Glen Elder, and Kenneth Keniston, among others, and formalized in theory by Urie Bronfenbrenner.

Most impressively, the author makes clear the connections between the family's social and economic situation and parental psychological characteristics—poor self-concepts, depressed moods, and emotional instability—which are reflected in aversive and often abusive interactions with the children, consequently endangering the children's welfare. In brief, the links in the causal chain leading to maltreatment of children are traced out, beginning with the social-structural features of the caregivers' environment, conditions that predispose them to use childrearing techniques that are destructive of their children's well-being, and inhibit or prevent the use of practices that enhance emotional, social, and cognitive development.

Fortunately, many families at high risk for child maltreatment are not actually abusive. Furthermore, as Baumrind indicates, some social context variables and interventions such as the presence of supportive family members or institutions, community solidarity, and parent education have frequently proven effective in buffering the effects of circumstances that often lead to child maltreatment. There is an urgent need for in-depth investigations of families who are at high risk but do not maltreat their children. Findings of such investigations may provide bases for further development of effective intervention techniques and welfare policies that would reduce the incidence of child maltreatment.

As often happens, Baumrind's extensive examination of pertinent information left her with as many questions as answers. In her final chapter, she generates a series of critical questions that must be systematically investigated before we can fully understand the etiology and prevention of the maltreatment of children. At the same time, her meticulous review, together with her vast knowledge about child development and socialization, enabled her to formulate sensible, practical recommendations for the establishment and implementation of policies that, at the very least, would help reduce the incidence of the conditions and circumstances that lead parents to abuse or neglect their children.

Two sensitive, well-written commentaries extend and enrich Baumrind's exposition by adding the perspectives of well-trained professionals who have had considerable experience working with families at high risk for child maltreatment. Jackson, a developmental psychologist, shows how some recent public policies have created social conditions and stresses in poor African American families that lead to an escalation of child punishment and abuse. These include inadequate financial support for dependent children, unwarranted placement of children in foster homes, discrimination and fragmentation of the extended family in public housing (because apartments in public housing projects are so small), and parent education practices that disparage African American culture. Jackson's penetrating analysis is the root of specific recommendations for ameliorative changes in public policy and the practices of welfare agencies.

Abrams, a former director of a welfare agency and an authority on the practices of those agencies, enthusiastically endorses the concept of scientific, research-based foundations for welfare practices and policymaking. Drawing on her long-term, intimate, practical experience, she also amplifies and concretizes a number of Baumrind's general recommendations for parent education, for broadening welfare workers' understanding of cultural differences, for designing effective programs to preserve families (rather than placing children in foster care), and for increased funding for programs designed to prevent child abuse.

The commentators' responses to Baumrind's essay are in themselves compelling evidence of the practical value of the scientist's scholarly and research work. In fact, the conceptualization, content, and structure of this impressive volume provide a model of how the social scientist can make significant contributions to the reduction of social ills and to the betterment of human welfare. It involves a sequence of events, beginning with the social scientist—preferably a recognized expert— defining the problem of concern carefully, and then attempting to discover its (always complex) determinants by thoroughly exploring the relevant research and theoretical literature, analyzing, evaluating, and integrating research findings. The goal of these activities is mapping the path from fundamental causes to specific effects. When this is accomplished, the expert can generate some tentative proposals about social interventions or social policies that would ameliorate or solve the problem. These, in turn, can be submitted to professionally trained people with broad, firsthand experience in dealing with the problem, its manifestations and consequences. Their assessments and suggested revisions can be incorporated by the social scientist, who can then present a set of sound, integrated recommendations.

The final successful product, illustrated by the present volume, has real potential for achieving the scientist's paramount goal: influencing policymakers and welfare officials to accept and implement practices that are "in the best interests of children." It is to be hoped that actions by appropriate authorities will make this potential a reality.

PREFACE

Diana Baumrind

I was commissioned by the National Academy of Science, Study Panel on Child Abuse and Neglect, to prepare a position paper on the family microsystem in the etiology of child maltreatment. My charge was to apply what we know about normative family functioning to the circumstances of abusive and neglectful families.

There are two worlds of childhood, separate and increasingly unequal. Researchers often fail to acknowledge how disparate these two worlds are, and therefore how little data derived from families in the world of the affluent can address the problems encountered by families in the world of the impoverished. As I reviewed the literature on child maltreatment, I was struck more by the dissimilarities than by the similarities between the two bodies of literature—one, familiar to me, derived from studies with predominantly healthy middle-class families concerned with the optimal development of their children's potentialities; the other, heretofore unknown to me, derived from observations of predominantly impoverished families where parents, of necessity, are absorbed in ensuring the survival of their children and themselves.

The majority of children who participated in my longitudinal investigation were brought up in safe and comfortable neighborhoods, and in middle-class families by parents who had the resources to guide their education and to provide them with good preventive medical care. By contrast, the majority of children and their parents who are *identified* as belonging to abusive or neglectful families lack the material resources that nourish growth and development—their own and their children's. They lack good medical care, are endangered by crime, and live in substandard homes situated in dilapidated neighborhoods.

Not all families exposed to high-risk settings succumb. Remarkably, the majority of families oppressed by similarly impoverished circumstances are not abusive or neglectful. Against great odds, many are able to provide their children with the emotional and spiritual sustenance that enables them not only to survive but to become healthy, productive members of society. Clearly, then, among those families who must cope with poverty there are parent and child personal attributes that distinguish maltreating from well-functioning members.

All parents, poor and nonpoor, who abuse or neglect their children must be held accountable for their acts of omission or commission. To treat adults because they are impoverished as nothing but victims of their circumstances is a misperception that adds insult to injury. Demands for responsible parenthood are empty rhetoric, however, without a concerted social commitment to reverse the gross inequality in the two worlds of children, an inequality recently widened in each succeeding generation in the United States.

In considering multiple pathways and interactive effects among the factors that contribute to child maltreatment, I could not help but be impressed by the preemptive destructive effects of the correlates of poverty on the rate of child maltreatment. The increasingly great disparity in the two worlds of children is the end result of public policies that mandate inequality in incomes, neighborhood security, school quality, and available preventive health care. The increasing inequality in the resources available to the affluent and the impoverished breeds violence, inside and outside the homes of those who are impoverished.

I conclude my review by offering some social policy recommendations intended to alleviate the correlates of poverty that encourage child maltreatment. I am keenly aware that I am not qualified by training or experience to specify how the research synthesis I provide might best be translated into public policy recommendations that could reduce the incidence of child maltreatment. For this guidance I turned to two experts intimately familiar with the population to be served: Jacquelyne Faye Jackson and L. Annette Abrams. Both commentators delineate the specific social institutional expressions of prejudice and poverty that in their experience have contributed to the escalation of child maltreatment. Each makes specific social policy recommendations directed to lawmakers and service providers. The contributions of these two articulate and well-informed African American scholars provide an invaluable perspective on how decision makers and field-workers should evaluate and utilize research findings pertaining to children, youth, and families.

Dr. Jackson, an esteemed colleague at the Institute of Human Development, agreed to share with the readers her letter to me identifying omissions in my review pertaining to specific public policies and social intervention practices that negatively impact on African American families, predisposing some to become abusers. In addition to her excellent academic credentials as a developmental psychologist earned at Stanford and the University of California at Berkeley, Dr. Jackson received her masters of social work in 1970 from the University of California and has worked in the community for many years as a school social worker, part of that time with adoption services for African American children.

Ms. Abrams is the former director of the Michigan Office of Children and Youth Services, and currently is associate director for policy of the Institute for Children, Youth, and Families at Michigan State University. She earned her bachelor of arts degree in politics and government from Howard University. Her professional career has been devoted to service in the areas of mental health, substance abuse prevention, and education. Ms. Abrams is eminently qualified to transform a scholarly literature review such as mine into a targeted social policy briefing for government agencies and social service providers.

My work referred to in this book has been supported generously by the William T. Grant Foundation. I also wish to acknowledge the continuing support of the Institute of Human Development and its current director, Professor J. J. Campos. The opinions expressed here are those of the author and do not necessarily reflect those of the National Academy of Science or its Study Panel.

Child Maltreatment and Optimal Caregiving in Social Contexts

CHAPTER ONE

Introduction

When C. Henry Kempe, F. Silverman, B. Steele, and associates (1962) created a new diagnostic entity—the battered child syndrome—medical legitimacy was given to the ubiquitous problem of child maltreatment. A plethora of federal funding programs, commission reports, specialized journals, research centers, and international societies and conferences were spawned to mount a frontal attack on potentially abusive, as well as already assaultive parents. Yet the problem of child abuse has not abated despite the considerable ongoing professional attention given to it, perhaps because the traditional support systems that enabled caregivers to cope with personal and social stressors in "kinder, gentler" times have broken down, and the times have become much harsher.

The position taken in this review is that escalating child maltreatment in the United States is symptomatic of societal abuse and neglect of the "forgotten half" of our citizens, with the primary causes and cures of child maltreatment attributable primarily to social-structural rather than to psychological factors. In chapter 2, I explore conceptual and empirical problems with definitions of child abuse and psychological maltreatment to illustrate the lack of consensus concerning what parental practices constitute maltreatment. In chapter 3, I identify some of the economic and cultural factors associated with child abuse in order to situate the abusive family within a larger social context. In chapter 4, I evaluate the importance of the relation to child maltreatment of such family context variables as maternal youth and inexperience, single-parent status, marital discord and divorce, adoptive or stepchild status, and the child's difficult behavior. In chapter 5, I consider such systems approaches to the study of normal and pathological family functioning as transactional models, developmental/organizational theory, and the burgeoning field of developmental psychopathology. In chapter 6, I examine the possible application to abusive families of important facets of the two major parenting dimensions of demandingness and responsiveness that describe normal parent-child relations, as well as patterns of parental authority based on these two dimensions. In chapter 7, I describe certain psychiatric and psychological attributes that have been posited to characterize abusive parents, and in that context evaluate the evidence for intergenerational transmission of abuse. Finally, in chapter 8, I offer some recommendations for prevention and intervention, and for research on child abuse. Two commentators, Jacquelyne Faye Jackson and L. Annette Abrams, discuss in greater depth the effects of prior and present child and family policies on social welfare recipients. Jackson critiques past and current social policies and programs as they affect African Americans. Abrams offers concrete recommendations for strengthening the fabric of the safety net provided to families in need.

The literature on child abuse and neglect is not well integrated with the literature on normal and optimal family functioning or socialization effects. There is a coherent body of literature and reasonable consensus about what constitutes high-quality parenting in middle-class, predominantly white populations. For such populations, the focus of examination is on styles of parenting and parental practices that generate different kinds and levels of competence, mental health, and character in normal children. By studying healthy, affluent, middle-class samples, thus eliminating the prepotent effects of prejudice, poverty, and chronic illness on children, the influence of variations in normal childrearing styles on child outcomes can be identified. By contrast, the vast and burgeoning research and clinical literature on child abuse and neglect, almost without exception, uses impoverished captive populations as subjects to assess the adverse effects of personal and social pathology on children. Because the two bodies of literature were collected for different purposes and on different populations, bridging them, although necessary, should be undertaken with caution.

Intergenerational transmission of poverty or privilege further divides the two kinds of subject populations—one subsisting, currently and in their families of origin, on public assistance under public scrutiny; the other, independent in their choice of lifestyle and shielded by affluence from intrusive examination. That children have the nominal right to protection from abuse and neglect, and in positive terms to love, health care, free education, opportunity to play, brotherhood, and freedom from discrimination, is seldom disputed today. By contrast to children's rights to protection, children's rights of choice are highly controversial. At one extreme, liberationists such as Farson (1974) and Holt (1974) and more recently Franklin (1986), applying civil rights rhetoric, claim for children rights equivalent to those of adults, such as the right to be free from any form of constraint by oppressive adults on their speech, choice of friends, and decorum, and even the right to enter into legally binding contracts. Child liberators view abrogation of these putative rights of choice as maltreatment. In the same vein, but more moderate, Gil (1975) regards any act of commission or omission by a caretaker or institution that deprives a child of equal rights and liberty or constrains the child's ability to achieve his or her optimal developmental potential as abusive. By contrast, philosophers such as Purdy (1992), and psychologists such as Baumrind (1978b), claim that dependent children have a right to care and protection, but not a right to the degree of autonomy accorded adults. Positioned at the extreme of this conservative position are religious fundamentalists, most notably by Dr. James Dobson of the Family Research Council in Colorado, whose advice is widely disseminated through radio and books. According to Lucier (1992), writing for the Family Research Council, the rights of individuals in the United States are established by God and as such take priority over policies set forth by civil law. Children have the right to protection, but not of choice, and their right to protection is balanced by their obligation to obey and respect their parents.

Thus, there is consensus in the United States that caregivers are obligated to protect children, but not that children have rights of choice that caregivers are obligated to respect. Even children's right to protection was not acknowledged until relatively recently, however. Throughout most of recorded history, children were literally the property of their fathers to be toyed with for amusement, chided and beaten for disobedience or misconduct, and put out to work at an early age. Authors of the two best-known books on the history of childhood, Phillippe Aries' *Centuries of Childhood* (1962) and Lloyd deMause's *History of Childhood* (1974), document routine treatment of children that today in this country would be categorized as abusive.

DeMause (pp. 51–54) describes six successive childrearing modes: (1) *infanticidal mode* (antiquity to fourth century A.D.), in which parents simply killed their unwanted or troublesome children; (2) *abandonment mode* (fourth to thirteenth centuries), in which unwanted or troublesome children, instead of being killed, were sent to a monastery, foster home, or service; (3) *ambivalent mode* (fourteenth to seventeenth centuries), in which children were allowed to enter into their parents' emotional life but only to be molded and beaten into a religiously mandated shape; (4) *intrusive mode* (eighteenth century), in which children were chastised more by guilt and threats, and less by beatings; (5) *socialization mode* (nineteenth to mid-twentieth centuries), in which children were trained to develop good habits (Skinner) and their impulses were directed and channeled (Freud) in the model of sociological functionalism; (6) *helping mode* (mid-twentieth century to 1974, when deMause published), in which parents were maximally responsive and gratifying, and minimally demanding and restrictive, on the assumption that the child knows better than the parent what it needs at each stage of its life. DeMause regarded the "helping" mode as epiphanic, and would have objected to having it supplanted by any other mode—even by Baumrind's *authoritative mode*, currently judged by many Western experts to be "best." In this mode parents direct their child's activities in a rational, issue-oriented manner, encourage verbal give and take, and share with the child the reasoning behind their guidelines, but exert firm control at points of divergence until the child in late adolescence can internalize the role of rational authority (Baumrind, 1966, 1971a).

Each childrearing mode described by deMause produced productive and accomplished individuals. Today, at least modes 4 through 7 (if one includes the authoritative mode) are sanctioned by some parents and subcultures in the United States. From the perspective of adherents of one mode, practices typical of another mode are deficient, if not downright abusive, so that there is no consensus concerning what common practices are to be treated by our pluralistic society as abusive.

CHAPTER TWO

Problems of Definition

The legislation establishing the National Center on Child Abuse and Neglect, adopting a value-neutral stance, defined child abuse (or maltreatment) by a caretaker as "physical or mental injury, sexual abuse, negligent treatment or maltreatment of a child under eighteen . . . which indicate that the child's health or welfare is harmed or threatened thereby" (PL 93–247, 93rd Cong. S1191). This definition fails to delineate "injury" or a "child's welfare," or to specify or evaluate cultural variations in what is meant by optimal development and good parenting. Recent attempts to define child abuse empirically have relied of necessity on Child Protective Services records (e.g., Cicchetti & Barnett, 1991), thus excluding the preponderance of middle-class families, and therefore the kinds of psychological "maltreatment" peculiar to their ecological niche, such as depriving preschoolers of the opportunity for self-directed play in order to accelerate their scholastic performance. An emerging phenomenon among adult children, primarily from middle-class families, is public acknowledgment of "recovered memories" of incest and child abuse that took place decades earlier, which are "remembered," generally in therapy and under hypnosis. The False Memory Syndrome Foundation has collected more than three thousand stories of adult children in therapy who recovered "memories" of abuse that may or may not have occurred. Unfortunately, these retrospective "data" on middle-class abuse are suspect, and prospective studies that could document incidence and kind of abuse occurring in middle-class families are nonexistent (Loftus, 1993). Similarly, we have no reliable information on the definition, incidence, and concrete manifestations of "psychological maltreatment."

9

Definitions of psychological maltreatment are especially ambiguous, as can be seen from the exchange between McGee and Wolfe (1991) and a spate of commentators, none of whom agree fully with the authors or with each other. The definition of "psychological maltreatment" proposed by McGee and Wolfe is any communication pattern that may potentially damage the child psychologically, especially by interfering with the child's resolution of important developmental tasks. Thompson and Jacobs (1991) argue that this definition is so broad that it could subject a wide spectrum of common parental practices to public scrutiny. Such common practices that some experts might regard as abusive include spanking and scolding, failure to provide psychological stimulation, inconsistent or coercive discipline, and humiliating the child.

Issues on which there was little consensus in the interchange among commentators on the McGee and Wolfe position paper are the following:

1. Should psychological maltreatment (for example, acts of terrorizing, rejection, isolation, missocialization, and exploitation) be separated from physical behaviors on the part of the parent that have physical effects on the child? Does frightening or isolating a child over a period of time endanger the child's mental health sufficiently to be labeled as psychological abuse and thereby to justify coercive intervention?

2. How does the developmental level of the child affect what acts are to be regarded as abusive? For example, most experts do not regard requiring an older adolescent to share fully in household tasks as exploitative, but do regard the same expectation of a seven-year-old as exploitative.

3. Should operational definitions of psychological maltreatment focus on outcome for the child, or solely on parents' acts, whatever their putative effects on the child?

4. Must the harm to the child be actual, or merely potential? For example, should lack of parental supervision be regarded as neglectful or psychologically uncaring only if the child is physically injured?

5. How disturbed, inconsistent, or insensitive does a parent have to be to be regarded as psychologically abusive, not merely as incompetent? Should demonstrably poor caregiving or dysfunctional parental conditions such as depression be regarded as maltreatment because of their probable negative effect on children's optimal functioning?

Most developmentally psychopathogenic acts of rejecting, degrading, missocializing, or exploiting the child, or reversing roles, or being emotionally unresponsive are manifestations of inadequate caregiving rather than of legally actionable abuse. The putative effects of these various kinds of psychological maltreatment can only be estimated probabilistically, as contrasted to the physical effects on the child of a severe beating or habitual neglect. For this reason, among others, Giovannoni (1991) concluded that "developmentally psychopathogenic" is a more appropriate term than "maltreatment" when the expected outcome of a caregiving practice is to generate psychopathology in the child, but the practice itself is not clearly outside the norms of conduct of the group or likely to entail substantial physical harm.

In sum: The research and social science communities continue to struggle with how child maltreatment, in particular psychological maltreatment, should be defined and identified. The current rash of "recovered memories" of parental sexual abuse by adults, usually women in therapy, further complicates the picture. As Goldstein, Freud, and Solnit (1979) concluded a decade ago, even if emotional neglect or maltreatment could be defined consensually, too little is known about how to intervene without doing more harm than good to justify coercive intervention. The stratum of society that protective services purports to serve does not trust its good intentions. Cultural variations in norms regarding the reciprocal rights and responsibilities of parents and children should be taken into account when determining which practices constitute maltreatment of sufficient degree to warrant legal intervention. A too broad and inclusive definition of child abuse threatens the perceived proprietary rights of parents, whereas a too narrow definition may fail to protect dependent children from truly abusive or neglectful parents.

CHAPTER THREE

The Family in Ecological Contexts

The primary caregiving unit—the family—is itself embedded in a complex ecosystem with socioeconomic factors of prime importance in the etiology of child abuse and neglect. The cultural context moderates the effects of family factors on children's development. The evolutionary context is thought by some scholars (most notably Belsky) to explain why it is "natural" under certain circumstances for some parents to abuse or neglect their children.

Evolutionary Context

From the evolutionary perspective enunciated by Belsky, Steinberg, and Draper (1991), child maltreatment evolved via natural selection in order to promote reproductively strategic characteristics in individuals exposed to stressful and harsh ecological contexts. Belsky (1980, 1993) and colleagues (with Steinberg & Draper, 1991; with Vondra, 1989) assert that, under certain conditions of limited resources, child abuse is as much a part of the natural condition in the animal (including human) world as is responsive, nurturing caregiving behavior. Belsky, Steinberg, and Draper (1991) posit that females who grow up under stressful conditions develop insecure attachments, and adopt the "r" reproductive strategy (producing many children who are poorly cared for) rather than the "K" strategy (rearing few offspring who are well cared for). Burgess and Conger (1978) had posited earlier that lack of parental resources decreases the probability of parental investment and bonding, thus increasing the risk of abuse (as does the status of being a stepchild, or an adopted, "damaged," or fragile child in a large family). According to these scholars, when social and economic resources are limited, parents will neglect or maltreat those of their children who are least likely to reproduce successfully, or who are biologically unrelated to them. When poverty, social isolation, and single parenthood coincide, allocation of resources to the care of "disposable" children undermines the reproductive prospects of the caregiver by siphoning off resources that could be used to rear healthy, biologically related children, present or potential. Children most likely to fall into this disposable category are handicapped, sickly, or premature infants, and adopted children or stepchildren who do not share their caregivers' genes.

Evolutionary explanations of abuse are thought by many (Baumrind, 1993; Gould, 1980; Lerner, 1992; Lewontin, 1991) to be unwarranted, with the evidence, such as it is, based on tenuous suppositions about reproductive strategies. Belsky himself points out (1993) that there are more straightforward psychological, sociological, and systems theories explanations than the need to replicate one's genes for the "evidence" sociobiologists have accrued to account for the admittedly strong association between poverty and child abuse. Circumstances associated with poverty that are cited by Belsky as favorable to the occurrence of abuse or neglect, such as multiple unplanned pregnancies closely spaced (Zuravin, 1988), handicap or illness, and younger age of child or mother, all have more parsimonious psychological or sociological explanations that do not invoke an unconscious drive to replicate. In the presence of poverty, abuse is overdetermined by conjoint stressors, including the likelihood of having a low birth weight baby who, due to the unavailability of contraceptive and abortive alternatives, was not planned or wanted. A vulnerable child (that is, one who is handicapped, sickly, or premature) further stresses limited family resources. The interrelated stressors that result from poverty, such as lack of social support, teenage motherhood, and low birth weight, suffice to explain poor-care parenting. The invocation by Belsky and his colleagues of the unconscious motive of reproductive fitness to explain the poverty-related circumstances associated with abuse is superfluous.

According to Gould (1980), the claim by sociobiologists that the genes that are retained universally in a species are adaptive is based on a collection of "just-so" stories about how the leopard got its spots or the rhino its wrinkled skin. Much sociobiological reasoning is teleological and not subject to refutation: If selection is taken as axiomatic, some adaptive value not open to scientific disconfirmation can always be construed post hoc. The scenarios Belsky and his colleagues propose to explain child abuse could or could not have taken place, and may or may not increase the fitness of those who engage in them. These scenarios cannot be disconfirmed by "exceptions" (that the majority of nonbiological parents are nonabusive) because these "exceptions" are conveniently attributed to reciprocal altruism (unrelated caregivers "give to get" resources that may in the future enhance the chances of their gene survival).

Sociobiological arguments by homology (parallels from nonhuman to human species) fail to take into account the unique characteristics of the human species, including intentional, self-conscious, agential behavior, and the manner in which human behavior is transformed by cultural existence (see Lerner, 1992; Lewontin, 1991). Humans are qualitatively different from other animal species at every level of integration—even at the simplest instinctual level. For example, when a nursing puppy chews its mother's nipple too hard she takes its entire head into her mouth and bites down until the puppy becomes still. Lacking a dog's instinct to communicate submissiveness to a dominant attacker, a human baby will cry and thrash about, rather than become passive and motionless. A human infant (unlike a puppy) would have no way of knowing how to placate an adult (or canine) abuser, and adult human abusers vary among themselves (as adult dogs do not) in what kind of communication from the child would put a halt to the abusive episode. Human emotions and motivation require cognitive appraisal of the meaning of a situation. Emotions such as anger and jealousy that can lead to abuse are not "elicited" in human beings, but rather are part of goal-directed and purposive behavior that is peculiarly human. Humans can feel pride in the accomplishments of their children and shame at not being able to provide for their wants, and these emotions aroused by purely human appraisals can give cause for abusing one's children, or for refraining from doing so. What human beings wish to reproduce in their children are their personal values, interests, and identifications. As a phylogenetically advanced species humans are uniquely capable of abstract, symbolic, complex, and deliberate appraisals of what is required of them to survive and flourish. Only humans can be intentionally humane as evidenced by the Christian rescuers of Jews during the Holocaust. Similarly, only humans (and possibly some higher apes) can be inhumane enough to brutalize vulnerable beings for perverse rather than survival ends. Acts of superogatory goodness are not reducible to "reciprocal altruism," or acts of brutality to the "selfish gene," but arise instead from moral and emotional attributes that are unique to the human species.

Despite Belsky's stated commitment to an ecological perspective, his theory is not one of social causation, but rather one of individual causation in which the structures of society merely reflect the inherently selfish predispositions of all individuals. Belsky and his colleagues assume (as though it were an established fact) that gene replication, not the peculiarly human motives of self-fulfillment, happiness, or meaning through contributing to the community, is the ultimate goal of human development. It is ironic that a psychologist who takes an evolutionary approach to human behavior would overlook phylogenetic development, by reducing the uniquely human aspects of love and planfulness in reproductive behavior to the zoomorphic motive of biological replication.

Economic Context

The status of American children and their families has clearly deteriorated in the past decade (Fuchs & Reklis, 1992; *Healthy Children: Investing in the Future*, 1988). The government-led outcry against parental abuse occurred simultaneously with what advocates of children's welfare decried as official sacrifice of children in public policy (Children's Defense Fund, 1991; Edelman, 1987; Steiner, 1981). As Garbarino (1990) has noted, the correlation between family income and child outcomes is higher in the United States than elsewhere in the Western world because the United States is almost unique among industrialized societies in failing to entitle all families to maternal and infant health care and to basic child-support subsidies. At least 3.6 million families are maintained by women with an income below the poverty level, with three-quarters of poor black families sustained solely by women (Pearce, 1990; Pelton, 1985). The abusive inequities suffered by the "forgotten half" in the United States (see *Final Report of Youth and America's Future, The William T. Grant Foundation Commission on Work, Family, and Citizenship,* 1988) include inadequate funding of such preventive and ameliorative services as AFDC, school lunches, food programs and subsidized medical care, and the foster child program. As a consequence of the deteriorating educational system, children's performance on standardized tests declined between 1960 and 1980 and then again between 1988 and 1991. Poverty-related homicide rates involving children and teenagers increased rapidly in the past decade, and the teenage suicide rate and *reported* rate of child abuse tripled in the decade ending in 1986.

Poor families are most subject to public scrutiny and thus to far higher officially reported rates of abuse and neglect than are middle-class families, with the possible exception of sexual abuse for which the reported class difference is not as great (Finkelhor, 1984). In the past few years the plethora of "recovered memory" recollections has added considerably to the reported incidence of middle-class incest and abuse. By comparing the incidence of child maltreatment reported to researchers working for the National Study of the Incidence and Severity of Child Abuse and Neglect, and official reports to protective services of these incidents, Hampton and Newberger (1985) concluded that families are most likely to be reported for child abuse when families are poor, the perpetrator is not the mother, maltreatment is not emotional, ethnicity is not white, and the nature of abuse is not sexual. There is consensus among field-workers and investigators both that the proportion of unreported to reported cases of child abuse is greater in middle-class suburbs than in inner-city ghettos, and that the relationship between economic privation and child maltreatment is not entirely artifactual. The most severe physical injuries occur in the poorest families (Gil, 1970), and the highest incidence of child neglect is found in families living in the most extreme poverty (Giovannoni & Billingsley, 1970). The circumstance associated with extreme poverty that most tragically affects children is homelessness. Families with children comprise one-third of the nation's homeless population (Children's Defense Fund, 1991); a conservative estimate finds one hundred thousand children homeless each night. It is not known whether the (reported) higher rates of child abuse or neglect among homeless women, compared with other poor families, is a product of their homelessness and extreme poverty, the result of substance abuse, or merely a reporting bias (Molnar, Rath, & Klein, 1990; Robertson, 1991). Some homeless women report that substance abuse coupled with domestic violence in their partner precipitated their homelessness (Dail, 1990). Although homeless women with dependent children have a lower rate of substance use and related problems than other homeless adults, the consequences of such abuse impair the mother's ability to compete for scarce resources and to allocate them to her offspring. The stresses of homelessness for children include violence, experienced and witnessed; dangers and disruptions presented by the shelters; difficulty in accessing health care and educational resources; and numerous traumatic losses, chronic adversities, and deprivations (Masten, 1992). Homeless children and their mothers generally endure hunger, insecurity, social isolation, elevated health problems (including infant mortality, low birth weight, immunization delays and infections), developmental delays, educational retardation, and behavioral and psychological problems. Homelessness is a psychological trauma and a caregiving stressor, placing mothers at risk for learned hopelessness and depression (Milburn & D'Ercole, 1991). Since homelessness is often treated as child neglect by protective services, the child may be placed in foster care; the homeless mother and child then suffer reduced contact with extended family members. Services that could combat the deprivations and developmental lags associated with homelessness that children suffer are woefully lacking, as are the educational and vocational opportunities required to enable their parents to become self-sufficient. (See the November 1991 issue of *American Psychologist* for a thorough review.)

The specific processes that mediate between unemployment or poverty and developmental risk are controversial. In their effort to identify the mediators of the effects of poverty on children Garbarino and Sherman (1980) contrasted two social environments, one high-risk and the other not, but with about the same level of poverty. They defined a high-risk poor neighborhood as one that is socially as well as economically impoverished. A socially impoverished environment contains few people who are free from "drain" (that is, whose resources exceed their needs), a generalized fear among its inhabitants of being exploited in neighborly interactions, and a high proportion of stressed and emotionally needy families. In a low-risk poor environment its inhabitants take pride in their neighborhood, care for their homes, provide security for their children, and respect each other. These family factors identified as buffers against poverty are unlikely to be present when parents and grandparents have not been gainfully employed. As the investigators expected, there was more child abuse in the high-risk poor neighborhood. Garbarino and Sherman demonstrate that not all economically impoverished families are equally impoverished socially. We have yet to explain, however, what personal and social resources enable an economically impoverished neighborhood to be relatively free from "drain." Likely social resources that could buffer the effects of poverty on family functioning, thus contributing to "low risk," include clean and decently maintained public housing, drug treatment programs for all fertile women, low levels of noise and air pollution, and police officers who walk their community beat. Perhaps most important are opportunities to be gainfully employed, with income supplemented if necessary, rather than supplanted, by government assistance.

Conger et al. (1992) proposed a family process model linking economic stress in family life to problematic and prosocial adolescent adjustment in 205 seventh-grade boys. Objective economic conditions, including unstable work, were related to parents' emotional state and behavior through their perceptions of increased economic pressure and limited resources to cope with that pressure. Economic stress generated depression and demoralization in parents, which in turn resulted in marital conflict and "bad" parenting—harsh, inconsistent discipline and hostile rejection or noninvolvement. Steinberg, Catalano, and Dooley (1981) found that reported child abuse and neglect increased after job loss. Lempers, Clark-Lempers, and Simons (1989) also found that the indirect effects of economic hardship worked through stress-induced changes in parental nurturance and discipline (as perceived by their adolescents). Similarly, Elder, Nguyen, and Caspi (1985) reported that severe income loss increased marital conflict, and also adversely influenced the psychosocial well-being of girls by increasing their fathers' rejection (especially of less attractive daughters). Mothers' behavior toward their children was not much affected in this study by economic hardship, but Elder (1974) has reported that when mothers lose respect for their husbands, as they often do when their spouses are unemployed, their sons do as well. For boys, economic hardship was linked to negative perception of their fathers and to psychological distress, and these associations were independent of paternal behavior, even though paternal harshness followed job loss.

Trickett et al. (1991) contrasted the childrearing practices of abusive and nonabusive impoverished families toward their four- to eight-year-old children. They examined data based on observations in the laboratory and home from two geographically separate maltreatment research projects (Harvard Child Maltreatment Project; NIMH Child Abuse Project), both of which had included a nonabusive comparison group. Subjects in both studies were drawn from urban or suburban populations. Neither of the two samples used a prospective longitudinal design, and results from neither apply to the rural poor or middle class. The NIMH and Harvard samples differed in important respects, including the extent to which the maltreatment and comparison groups were well matched. In the NIMH project, the maltreatment families differed substantially from the comparison group on certain demographic variables, although both groups were poor: Maltreatment families were predominantly urban rather than suburban, single-parent rather than two-parent, and welfare-dependent rather than working but poor. Because of these substantial differences in ecological factors it is not surprising that the differences between abusive and nonabusive poor families with regard to childrearing practices and outcomes were much larger for the NIMH sample than for the Harvard sample. Across both groups, abusive parents had less access to family support and community resources. They experienced less pleasure and displayed more negative affect toward their children, perceiving their children as displaying more problem behavior. The form of control used by abusive compared to nonabusive poor parents was more authoritarian and they did not encourage their children's autonomy. Neither race nor marital status predicted these childrearing variables. Socioeconomic status (SES) related positively to parents' encouragement of autonomy and negatively to their use of authoritarian control for both abusive and nonabusive parents. SES related positively to enjoyment of the parental role only for the nonabusive comparison group.

The overwhelming negative effects of extreme poverty on the quality of parenting is evident from these studies. Childrearing practices and child outcomes were most unfavorable in the lowest socioeconomic groups where the differences between abusive and nonabusive families were not discernible. Differences in both childrearing practices and child outcomes between abusive and nonabusive families were apparent only for the higher-income poor families.

The following childrearing factors have been proposed as possible mediators in these and other studies of the effects of poverty on children's socioemotional functioning.

Greater reliance on power-assertive disciplinary procedures. Numerous studies document the greater tendency of low-income caregivers to use physical discipline, issue commands without explanation, not consult with their children, not reward their children verbally, and not discipline them supportively (e.g., Conger et al., 1984; Gecas, 1979; Wilson, 1974). Stressful events take their toll, even in well-to-do families (Weinraub & Wolf, 1983), but more so when the "hassles" are chronic, as they are for the urban poor. The excessive use of power-assertive discipline may be an expression of stress and the need to feel empowered in the home when other channels to social status are blocked. A sense that the environment is out of control may lead parents to distance themselves from their children, or alternatively to be overcontrolling by means of power-assertive techniques of discipline. Primary reliance on power-assertive techniques of discipline impacts negatively on children's willingness to cooperate and on their cognitive development (Hoffman, 1963, 1970b).

Greater negative parental affect (hostility, depression, irritability). Although the gap between the very rich and the very poor has increased in the past decade, the belief is perpetuated in the United States that all citizens are entitled to the physical amenities of life. A sense of entitlement in the face of society's neglect is likely to generate frustration and rage, as well as depression and despair in the chronically poor, contributing to their high rate of violence inside as well as outside the home. Parents respond to uncontrollable economic loss with a sense of helplessness, hopelessness, and alienation, which in turn is associated with physical and verbal abuse as well as less maternal sensitivity. Often as a result of their own neediness and immaturity, maltreating parents are in competition with their children for care and attention, and these unmet needs increase under the stress of poverty. Poverty also impedes easy access to family planning services so that an infant born to a poor mother is less likely to have been planned and therefore welcomed.

Children of poverty, whether or not they have been abused, are often depressed, anxious, and fearful; their homes, whether or not they are abusive, are often disorganized, apathetic, and stressful, and situated in neighborhoods that are violent and dangerous (Elmer, 1977). Young children of depressed parents show similar socioemotional problems as economically deprived children, with these two risk factors for child neglect highly associated.

More conflictual marital relations. Economic stress frequently results in demoralization, which in turn leads to marital conflict (Conger et al., 1992) and divorce. Divorce is generally followed by further economic loss (Hetherington, Stanley-Hagan, & Anderson, 1989), precipitating deeper maternal depression and subsequent neglect, as well as dissension in the parent dyad. Dissension in the parent dyad often precipitates conflictual parent-child relations (Herrenkohl & Herrenkohl, 1981), which may escalate to abuse.

A greater tendency to maltreat difficult children. In economically deprived populations temperamentally difficult children are more likely to be selected as targets of parental maltreatment (Elder, Caspi, & Nguyen, 1986; Rutter, 1979). Under stressful conditions associated with poverty, escalating cycles of parent-child conflict and aggression are easily triggered by children's defiance or irritability.

Higher negative attributions. Parents who rate their children as aggressive and hyperactive, when home observers cannot detect such differences, are more likely to be abusive (Reid, Kavanaugh, & Baldwin, 1987). Lower-income parents are more likely than other parents to attribute children's misbehavior to willfulness or stubbornness, and therefore to discipline their children harshly.

Environmental factors that enhance network embeddedness have been found to buffer the negative effects of poverty. These include the following.

Family solidarity. Solidarity within the family enhances family members' sense of security. Elder Nguyen, and Caspi (1985) reported that during the Great Depression, a sense of effectance and competence could be generated in children by mutual engagement with parents in work and household chores. The presence of a stable partner or a compatible grandmother has been found to be an important source of emotional support for primary caregivers in poor families (Furstenberg, Brooks-Gunn, & Morgan, 1987; Kellam, Ensminger, & Turner, 1977). Emotional support from their own mothers has been found to decrease poor adolescent mothers' hostility and indifference toward their children (Colletta, 1981).

Neighborhood cohesion. Well-organized neighborhoods with caring neighbors who show respect for each other appear to buffer the effects of poverty (Garbarino & Sherman, 1980). Maltreating families also tend to be a source of drain to other families, however, taking more than they give when they interact at all (Crittenden, 1985a; Polansky et al., 1981). The fact that many maltreating families are transient (Creighton, 1985; Zuravin, 1988), and do not use available community resources

(Giovannoni & Billingsley, 1970; Starr, 1988) suggests that maltreating parents may contribute intentionally to their own isolation. Thus, the greater isolation of abusive families may not be a direct result of poverty, but instead a consequence of their poor social functioning that interacts with the effects of poverty to generate isolation.

Social networks that parents find supportive. By monitoring the caregiving of mothers in distress, indigenous support lessens poor parents' tendency to engage in punitive, coercive discipline (Cochran & Brassard, 1979; Wilson, 1989). The indigenous support systems within a community provided by informal foster care, the church, and political leaders should therefore be cultivated. Abusive parents may select social networks that support their maladaptive parenting styles, however, in which case their social network will not act as a protective factor.

Despite the fact that most poor parents do not maltreat their children, poverty is the single most important predictor of parental maltreatment; it directly harms children's development by depriving them of essential material and psychological resources, and stresses their caregivers so as to render them less efficacious and more irascible and depressed. Economic privation magnifies the adverse effects on parents of such negative child personality attributes as poor impulse control, and the effects on children of such negative family structure variables as divorce and adoptive status.

Subcultural Context

Members of various subcultures in the United States do not agree on which practices are abusive. The patterns of childrearing that generate competence vary among cultures and historical periods. Just as the definition of optimal competence varies with the culture, the optimal balance of freedom and control varies with the modal level of stability of the larger society within which the family is embedded. Because the social structure in which families are embedded has become increasingly unstable over the past forty years, there has been a correspondingly increased need for structure, engagement, and discipline in the family context (Bronfenbrenner, 1985).

Although normative standards concerning acceptable childrearing practices vary across cultures, within each culture members distinguish between benign and harmful practices, and identify abusive practices that diverge from cultural norms. Cultural childrearing norms may provide an excuse for some parents to neglect or abuse their children (Hauswald, 1987). For example, among the Navajo, children are given great responsibility for herding sheep and performing other helpful tasks, including the care of younger siblings. Many drug- or alcohol-addicted mothers carry this transfer of responsibility to an older child to an extreme, however, failing to provide adequate supervision or sustenance, a practice that is condemned by the norms of Navajo culture. Similarly, the standards that her Palestinian American father attempted to enforce with Tina Isa were culturally dictated, but the sentence of death he imposed on her when she flouted his authority violated the norms of most Palestinian American parents.

All cultures have criteria for identifying sexual acts that fall outside the range of acceptability and will proscribe such behavior. The same cultures that accept fondling young children's genitalia to soothe them or to express pride, proscribe similar fondling of older children, or treating the child as a tool for the gratification of adults (Korbin, 1987). Sexually abusive acts in any culture can be recognized by the extreme secrecy with which they are conducted and the disruption they create in culturally expected roles, relationships, and behaviors between caregiver and child. Ahn and Gilbert (1992) report that the proportion of females who claim to have been sexually abused as children range from as low as 6% to as high as 62%, a range whose breadth may be due in part to varying cultural norms and to historical changes in what behaviors constitute sexual abuse in the study populations. Ahn and Gilbert reported that European Americans and African Americans had in common the most stringent standards regarding parent-child physical intimacy. Asian immigrants (with some exceptions such as the Vietnamese who regard women as polluting) consistently favored parent-child co-bathing to a later age than other ethnic groups.

Members of Asian, compared to European American and African American subcultures, however, considered parental expressions of affection as inappropriate for children to observe. Some Filipino nannies regarded fondling and masturbating young children in their care as appropriate means of soothing. In Korean and Vietnamese cultures a grandfather's touching a young boy's genitals is typically regarded as an expression of adoration and pride. Yet, as Ahn and Gilbert state, immigrants from these countries were prosecuted for such sexual "crimes" in the United States.

Exemplifying cultural differences in values concerning optimal childrearing practices and child outcomes, Japanese mothers have developed an indulgent, harmonious mother-child relationship that by Western standards is imbalanced in favor of responsiveness over demandingness. Their ideal childrearing style is intended to generate their ideal adult character. In sharp contrast to American ideals, Japanese mothers attempt to encourage a culturally syntonic strong need for approval and sense of dependence on fiduciaries (amae), and an imbalance in the communion/agency ratio favoring communion (Azuma, 1986).

In addition to their disproportionate representation among the unemployed and impoverished, African American families are subject to mundane extreme environmental stress from overt racism and oppression, chronic devaluation, and eruptions of racially based crises (Peters & Massey, 1983). To the extent that child abuse is a response to stress and a sense of powerlessness, and neglect is a reaction of helplessness on the part of parents who find themselves unable to provide for their children, one would expect child maltreatment to occur disproportionately among African American families when compared to European American families. Although the incidence of abuse by African American caregivers is generally reported as greater than by European American or Asian American parents, some investigators (e.g., Cazenave & Straus, 1979) conclude that, after controlling for socioeconomic status, African Americans are less likely to abuse their children.

The theoretical reviews of McLoyd (1990; McLoyd & Wilson, 1990) illumine the family processes that affect the socioemotional functioning of children living in very poor black families. Several results from the McLoyd and Wilson study that at first glance appear counterintuitive have important implications, provided they can be replicated: The more efforts mothers made to balance family needs and income, the more distressed they became, and the more they discussed their problems with their children; children's distress was positively associated with such discussions, and also with more social support from nonrelatives, especially from professionals. These results suggest that interventions not attuned to the special circumstances and values of the recipients are likely to backfire, and that certain efforts by impoverished women to cope with their extremely difficult circumstances, by increasing their level of stress and frustration, may increase rather than alleviate their distress.

Most American parents admit to hitting their children, but according to Alvy (1987) the proportion of black parents who resort to physical punishment is somewhat higher—99% compared to 95% of white low-income families and 82% of white higher-income families. Whereas 40% of the higher-income whites felt ambivalent about hitting, only 12% of low-income black parents experienced such reservations. Reasons given by black parents for hitting their children include to improve their behavior, to teach respect and obedience, and to directly change behavior during early childhood when their children's language is limited. The high value placed on obedience and respect for authority by African American families that can result in ready use of corporal punishment has been traced to African tradition by some scholars (Kohn, 1977; Peters, 1976; Young, 1970). Black parents may resort to restrictive, coercive, or punitive tactics strategically to protect children from the dangers that surround them in inner cities, and to foster the aggressiveness and guardedness needed for their children's survival in hostile environments (McLoyd, 1990; Ogbu, 1981). Although strict discipline and the use of corporal punishment do not (in my view) constitute "violence" or child abuse, frequent initial resort to such practices may predispose some parents to excuse assaulting a child under "triggering" contexts that arouse parental anger and frustration. Parents who rely more than necessary on hitting may be encouraged by home visitors to ascribe more child-oriented motives, such as neediness, to behavior previously interpreted as defiant and thus justifying harsh punishment, and to use such alternative disciplinary methods as "time-out" more frequently. Culturally sensitive parent education is often welcomed by poor black parents.

Protective features of the African American family include a church community that looks after the welfare of its parishioners, and an extended kinship network that gives close friends as well as family members rights over children, including the right to take children from their biological parents and foster them in times of crises (Martin & Martin, 1978; Stack, 1974). The church and religious life remain a major strength of the black family and a potential agency of intervention when abuse occurs. Frequently social support service requirements interfere with such culturally sanctioned protective strategies by removing the child to a "healthier" rural environment, or refusing to provide the mother (or indigenous child caregiver) with support unless the child is living with its mother and its father is absent from the home. Although the female-headed family has replaced the nuclear family as the modal family type among African Americans (Edelman, 1987), black fathers, when present in the home, have historically been observed to share the expressive, nurturant aspects of child care (Hill, 1972). Therefore, partners of black mothers are a present or potential resource as nurturers, a resource that caseworkers and program designers should consider utilizing more fully.

Unfortunately, the extended kinship network that has historically functioned as a safety net for black families has been decimated by two factors that disproportionately affect African Americans: crack cocaine addiction in mothers and the AIDS epidemic. Whereas middle- and upper-socioeconomic status (SES) pregnant women use alcohol and marijuana as frequently as lower-SES women, their cocaine use is much lower (Chasnoff, Landress, & Barrett, 1990; Schutzman et al., 1991). Crack cocaine addiction has undermined the capacity of many poor, black mothers to parent. In addition, gay black men who in the past were a resource for their siblings with children are now a drain when they contract AIDS. Thus, the extended kinship network is not currently performing the protective function for black youth to the extent that it has in the past, increasing the need for primary prevention services and for identifying and serving the special needs of drug-exposed children and their families. (For a different perspective, see Jackson's commentary.)

Radical cultural relativists question whether any form of parent-child relations judged by a society to be a necessary subsistence strategy or a cultural artifact should be labeled as abusive. For example, should infanticide practiced today with unwanted female infants in rural North India or sickly babies among the Tarahumara Indians of Mexico (Scheper-Hughes, 1987) be regarded as maltreatment? An open-minded appreciation of cultural differences concerning ethical values is essential in evaluating the childrearing practices or customs of a culture not one's own. Cultural pluralism by contrast with radical relativism mandates understanding and respect, not unconditional acceptance. Members of a host culture may apply a generalizable norm, like proscribing practices that protect the status quo at the expense of the disempowered, provided that the norm is applied equitably. An example is female circumcision, practiced in some African tribes to keep women subservient. In accord with the premium we place on human rights it is appropriate in our culture to forbid immigrants to practice female circumcision, while appreciating the differences in values that make the practice acceptable to the indigenous culture. By contrast, the ritual killing of animals in religious ceremonies by the Santeria, although repellent to most members of the majority culture in the United States, cannot ethically be proscribed by a mainstream culture that permits animals to be slaughtered for clothing and sport.

Summary

The great harm inflicted on children and their parents by being raised poor in the midst of plenty is acknowledged by all scholars concerned with the etiology of child abuse, including those who adopt sociobiological explanations for how poverty motivates parents to selectively abuse a child. Extreme poverty directly impacts children and their parents by depriving them of physical sustenance and appropriate conditions in which to learn and develop. Although poverty is not a sufficient or necessary antecedent for child abuse or neglect by parents, poverty generates stressful experiences and anger that can easily precipitate less than optimal caregiving, if not maltreatment. When compared to affluent parents, poor parents, even those who are not abusive, are more likely to be authoritarian, unsupportive, unresponsive, contentious, irritable, and depressed, and to perceive their children as willfully defiant and difficult. Network embeddedness, culturally attuned social support services, and a neighborhood relatively free from social "drain" may buffer, but not neutralize, the negative effects of poverty on children.

The cultural context must be taken into account when labeling parents' behavior as abusive, or when attempting to change their childrearing practices. Thus, the use of corporal punishment by African American parents should not per se be labeled as abusive, or the touching of young children's genitals by loving caregivers, as sexually exploitative.

To attribute biological function, as in survival and reproductive success, to human behavior does not signify that the behavior pattern is inevitable. Particular behavior patterns develop only under certain environmental conditions. The environmental condition most strongly associated with child abuse is extreme poverty. Interventions intended to support parents must target directly the poverty-related social-structural factors that cause hopelessness and helplessness by constraining parents' ability to provide a healthy home environment. The mechanisms invoked by Belsky and his colleagues to explain how poverty leads to abuse are no different from those more traditional sociologists, psychologists, and psychopathologists have already proposed, except that the tenuous motive of a largely unconscious need to reproduce one's own genes is needlessly attached. Sociobiological explanations for child abuse add nothing to our understanding of how to prevent or treat maltreatment, nor are they needed to advance our understanding of how poverty degrades the home environment and parents' willingness and ability to provide high-quality care for their children.

CHAPTER FOUR

Family Contexts of Child Maltreatment

Circumstances that diminish caregivers' capacity to nurture and are associated with a higher incidence of child abuse include maternal youth and inexperience, single-parent status, marital discord and divorce, adoption, and having a difficult child (Parke & Collmer, 1975).

Maternal Youth and Inexperience

The transition to parenthood, in middle-class as well as working-class families, is often accompanied by a decrease in marital satisfaction and an increase in conflict (Cowan & Cowan, 1992). However, being single, young, black, and poor is the combination of factors most likely to be associated with lack of marital fulfillment and poor caregiving in new mothers (Egeland & Erickson, 1987). Inexperienced caregivers who are unskilled in detecting an irritable infant's signals may inadvertently reinforce persistent crying by failing to respond to low-intensity cues and responding only when the infant escalates its demands with high-intensity cues. Younger mothers are less prepared to cope with the lifestyle changes a baby fosters. Older mothers are more likely to be married, to have planned their pregnancy, and to be better prepared for the rigors of motherhood.

Despite the overall decrease in the adolescent birthrate (because fully half of teenage pregnancies are terminated by abortion [Chilman, 1983]), the rate of babies born to unmarried compared to married teenagers and the percentage of unmarried teenagers who keep their babies have both increased (Furstenberg, Lincoln, & Menken, 1981; Hamburg & Dixon,

1992). Young people may view children as symbolic of generativity when being productive through work is not an attainable goal. Inner-city black youth may therefore feel ambivalent about using contraceptives to prevent pregnancy (Zabin, Astone & Emerson, 1993).

Although some investigators (Elmer, 1967; Gil, 1970) find no evidence of a relation between parental age and child abuse, others (e.g., Lynch & Roberts, 1977) report a much higher incidence of abuse by teenage mothers. Several studies indicate that adolescent mothers are more afraid of "spoiling" their babies (e.g., Wise & Grossman, 1980) and express more punitive childrearing attitudes than older women from similar lower-class backgrounds (Field et al., 1980). Adolescent mothers may turn to their babies for love and therefore be spontaneously demonstrative and affectionate, yet inattentive and unresponsive to their infants' bids for attention. The higher incidence of morbidity of children of adolescent mothers is thought by some investigators (e.g., Newberger, Melnicoe, & Newberger, 1986) to be a function of the presence of an abusive young male in the home, and the complex of factors associated with poverty, rather than of maternal age. Poorer mothers are more likely to be younger. Adolescent mothers who are also poor and single (as in fact most are) are more likely to mistreat their infants. Kinard and Klerman (1980) concluded from their review that most studies of adolescent mothers, whatever their findings, are spurious because of the uncontrolled association of social class with both teenage pregnancy and child abuse.

The baby's father and the mother's mother can each play an essential role in providing support for the adolescent mother (Crockenberg, 1987), thus relieving her perceived stress due to loneliness, overwork, or having an irritable infant, and thereby decreasing the likelihood that she will abuse her baby. Crnic et al. (1983) reported that mother's satisfaction with the status of her intimate support, especially from her husband, enhanced her satisfaction with parenting and her synchronous responsiveness with her infant. Day-to-day assistance and emotional support, especially from partners, is also found to be associated with a higher sense of mastery and self-esteem in inexperienced mothers (Belle, 1982; Turner & Noh, 1983), especially those who are poor. According to Turner and Noh, only 20% of the women in their study who had both high intimate support and a sense of mastery were of lower-class status. Yet for those women who fell in the upper half of both distributions of being the recipient of intimate support and having a sense of mastery, no relation was found between socioeconomic status and psychological distress. Thus, the few young women fortunate enough to have strong support from their own mothers, and who are mature, are often competent caregivers, despite being young and poor.

When the expectations young mothers have for emotional support during a crisis are unmet by professional caseworkers, or intimates are domineering, their "helpfulness" incurs too great a cost and is not associated with mothers' sense of well-being (McLoyd & Wilson, 1990). In a long-term follow-up of three hundred low-income teenage mothers in inner-city Baltimore, Furstenberg (1976) found that young mothers did much better over time if they remained in their parents' home, but not if they left and then returned, presumably because they then resented maternal intrusiveness. For the young Mexican American mothers in Colletta's sample (1981), perceived daily support was associated with smiling and eye contact in mothers' interactions with their infants. Many of the young mothers in her study evaluated the professional advice they received as intrusive and domineering, in which case such advice was rejected and experienced as causing, rather than relieving, stress.

Single-Parent Status

Children raised by a single parent, whether from white middle-class families or disadvantaged backgrounds, are somewhat more likely to drop out of school, to become teen mothers, and if they should marry, to divorce their husbands. For the average white child, being reared by a single parent appears to eliminate many of the advantages associated with being white, probably because of the loss of income and access to social resources (McLanahan, 1994).

Some scholars believe that children who lack two parents of the opposite sex will experience a disruption in normal psychosexual development. From a Freudian perspective, normal sex-typed identity requires the presence of two opposite-sexed parents, in order that children may learn gender-appropriate behavior from their same-sex parent and understand opposite-sex behavior. It has been noted that children, particularly early maturing girls raised by single, divorced mothers, frequently became prematurely emancipated, resulting in a higher rate of risk-taking behavior. Girls raised by single divorced mothers are more forward with males (Hetherington, 1972), which may lead to early adolescent sexuality. The growth in the number of one-parent and same-sex parents provides investigators with an opportunity to test assumptions about the putative negative effects of growing up without two parents of the opposite sex.

Many investigators have tied single parenthood to maltreatment (e.g., Gil, 1970; Spearly & Lauderdale, 1983); other investigators (e.g., Murphy, Orkow, & Nicol, 1985) find no such association. Blechman (1982) claims that there are many methodological problems with studies of psychological risk in single-parent households. These include reporter bias: Teachers' ratings generally favor children from two-parent families, but do not agree highly with objective measures of the children's attributes. Blechman's other methodological criticisms of the literature on adverse child outcomes in single-parent households include: (1) confusion of cause with effect (for example, children's maladjustment may precede, and contribute to, divorce rather than be caused by it; see Block, Block, & Gjerde, 1986); (2) confounds with low income and social status; (3) failure to control for cause of parental absence and level of emotional support; (4) inadequate consideration of the developmental status at which the child is studied; (5) ratings biased by welfare status of parent; and (6) failure to include measures of possible strengths as well as weaknesses of single-parent families. Blechman contends, and Gelles (1989) confirms, that with the effects of poverty, minority status, and recency of divorce controlled, there are few additional effects of single-parent status on the incidence of child maltreatment or of other adverse child outcomes. After the initial adjustment period, they contend, many single parents, who do not suffer the added burdens of poverty and prejudice, rear children quite adequately.

Marital Discord and Divorce

The negative effects of divorce per se must be separated from the negative effects of the dramatic decline in financial status and altered disciplinary practices that often, but need not, accompany divorce. Most available studies of divorce are based on white well-educated families with many studies relying on a clinical or legally embroiled sample. The well-known work on the negative effects of divorce, *Second Chances* by Wallerstein and Blakeslee (1989), used no comparison groups to differentiate between general secular effects and the specific effects of divorce.

In his definitive review of the relation between marital disputes and behavior problems in children, Emery (1982) concluded that interparental discord, not divorce, provides the principal explanation for the association between divorce and ongoing childhood problems. The quality of family relations, according to Hetherington et al. (1992), is an important mediator of children's responses to their parents' remarriage or divorce. Marital distress frequently results in subsequent deficiencies in caregiving (Cowan & Cowan, 1992). Marital discord weakens the parental alliance in disciplining and guiding their children. Just-divorced or just-remarried mothers become less authoritative—that is, less supportive and less effective at monitoring their children's activities. Thus, divorced mothers in the Cowans' study tended to engage with their sons in what Patterson (1982) refers to as the "fight cycle"—angry, escalating, coercive behavior. Mothers did not track their sons' behavior, or reinforce them consistently and contingently, and thus their disciplinary efforts were ineffectual.

Whether marital conflicts affect children adversely depends in part on the extent to which parents' quarrels are hateful, violent, and child-related. Children's ability to regulate their emotions and behavior is disrupted by strong and frequent emotional arousal (Grych & Fincham, 1990). Because marital conflicts tend to be highly arousing to children who observe them, children exposed frequently to such conflicts often become sensitized to any expression of parents' anger, responding with escalating expressions of distress or anger (Cummings & Zahn-Waxler, in press). Witnessing spousal conflicts involving physical aggression is especially traumatic for children (Cummings, Ballard, & El-Sheikh, 1991). When interadult conflicts not involving physical violence are resolved, ending in friendly interaction, children's feelings of distress are greatly reduced (Cummings, Iannotti, & Zahn-Waxler, 1985). Being present during aggressive interparental conflict may also affect children indirectly. By directing their attention toward the child and thus away from each other, quarreling parents inadvertently reinforce children's misbehavior that is instigated to distract them. In addition, children may emulate parents' aggressive maneuvers (Emery, 1982). When marital conflicts are child-related, children experience greater feelings of self-blame and fear of becoming involved (Emery, 1982). Marital conflicts are unlikely to result in physical child abuse unless spousal battering is present. Parents who are violent with each other, however, often also mistreat their children (Belsky, 1980; Garbarino, 1976).

The period surrounding divorce is particularly acrimonious, and a transitional period of disengagement and disruption in parenting is common (Hetherington et al., 1992). The early postdivorce period may be stressful and chaotic because, in addition to increased parental conflict, the custodial parent frequently changes residence, works longer hours, and makes new child care arrangements. As a consequence, the recently divorced parent often has a diminished capacity to discipline supportively or to respond sensitively to the needs of the child (Wallerstein, 1985).

Normally, the marital relationship provides the primary support system for parents (Belsky & Vondra, 1989). The sensitivity of a supportive husband to his wife's emotional distress can reduce not only her distress but buffer its disruptive effects on the child. Discord or divorce may negatively impact the child by removing the primary caregiver's spousal support at a time when she is extremely distressed. Role diffusion and role reversal may accompany marital discord or separation, with children seduced into parenting their parents (Johnston, 1990). As has been reported with the effects of child maltreatment, a particularly good relationship with at least one parent, or even a close parent surrogate, can mitigate, but not eliminate, the effects of marital turmoil on children.

The evidence concerning possible sex-differentiated effects of divorce is inconclusive. In general, interparental conflict appears to be related more strongly in boys to problems of undercontrol than of overcontrol (e.g., Block, Block, & Morrison, 1981; Hess & Camara, 1979). Conduct problems may be a function of modeling by boys of their fathers' aggressive behavior toward their mothers. Boys tend to be exposed to greater parental conflict, both because discordant parents are more likely to remain married when they have a son, and because parents are less willing to fight in front of daughters (Hetherington, Cox, & Cox, 1982). Stepparents and paramours are overrepresented as perpetrators of most kinds of abuse (Gelles & Harrop, 1991), and especially of sexual abuse toward girls (Finkelhor, 1984). Hetherington concluded that whereas boys experience more conflictual, coercive relations with their custodial mothers, girls, especially during adolescence, have more trouble adjusting to mothers' remarriage.

Adoption and Stepfamily Status

The rate at which adopted children and stepchildren are referred to mental health facilities for a variety of psychological and school-related problems is much greater than their representation in the general population (Bowman & Sigvardsson, 1990). Although in their initial reports Hetherington, Cox, and Cox (1985) found more acrimonious relations between stepfathers and stepdaughters, in their later publication (1992) Hetherington et al. reported that the gender difference (from the perspective of the stepfathers and other adults) tended to occur in the opposite direction, with girls seen as more competent. The high incidence of psychological problems in adopted children is not due primarily to physical abuse, since adoptive parents are carefully selected and monitored and generally not poor. Sexual abuse is more common in adoptive and stepfamilies, however, than in the intact biologically related family, with the absence of blood ties used by perpetrators to rationalize sexual seductions (Easson, 1973).

Sociobiologists such as Belsky (1980; with Steinberg & Draper, 1991) and Burgess and Draper (1989) claim that caregivers are likely to be less solicitous toward children whose genes do not replicate their own. They assert that the greater risk of child abuse associated with adoptive or stepfamily status derives from ancient, largely unconscious evolutionary processes. The fact that most adoptive, foster, or stepparents do not abuse or neglect their children is attributed by Belsky and his colleagues to "reciprocal altruism." There is, however, no tangible evidence to support this speculation. Also one must question why fertile persons would ever choose to foster or to adopt biologically unrelated children if their prime motive for doing so is biological replication. Rather than abuse or neglect adopted or stepchildren, adults could enhance their reproductive fitness by simply declining to adopt or to become a stepparent to children not biologically related to themselves.

The disruptions in caregiving that are often found in adoptive families may be due primarily to insecure attachment and incompatibility. Attachment theory suggests that a child placed after six to eight months of age may be unable to develop a secure attachment to a primary caregiver. Compatibility problems can occur because adoptive parents, when compared to biological parents, are less similar to their children in physique, personality, and intellect, and may even be from a different race. When major mismatches occur, adoptive parents and children are likely to have less intuitive understanding of each other, and so to feel less close emotionally. The greater likelihood that parents will abuse or neglect stepchildren may be explained by stress-generating factors such as jealousy of the relationship between the child and his or her biological parent, stigma associated with being a stepparent, absence of early bonding experiences, and the greater difficulty of being sensitive and responsive to a child who does not resemble oneself. Sociobiological speculations are superfluous.

Difficult Children

Rutter (1987) has proposed that children with difficult temperaments are more likely to both elicit, and be the target of, aversive responses from parents, especially when parents are stressed, as during a period of marital conflict or separation. Poor parenting skills and inappropriate expectations of the child, together with what Polansky, Borgman, and DeSaix (1972) call the "apathy futility" syndrome, are implicated in neglect. Although children's own behavior may precipitate or perpetuate maltreatment, it is unlikely to be its primary cause. Neither abused nor neglected children have been found to emit more initiating aversive behavior than well-treated controls (Burgess & Conger, 1978; Wolfe, 1985). Yet abusive parents report more problem behavior than objective observers perceive (Reid, Kavanaugh, & Baldwin, 1987), suggesting that abusive parents may be hyperreactive.

Infants who are irritable and hard to soothe may incite hyperreactive caregivers to disengage (Bell & Ainsworth, 1972; Robson & Moss, 1970). Many studies report an association between low birth weight and child abuse (e.g., Fontana, 1968; Klein & Stern, 1971). Explanations for the association include the mother's disappointment with the child's progress, greater demands made by the infant of its mother, postnatal separation that interferes with bonding, and less infant responsiveness to the mother's overtures. The relation between low birth weight and abuse, however, appears primarily when mothers are also impoverished, not supported emotionally, and ill-informed. For example, Crnic et al. (1983) did not find low birth weight to be associated with abuse. Unlike most such studies, their premature and comparison infants were well matched, healthy, and predominantly from middle-class families.

The older child may elicit abuse from susceptible parents by escalating disciplinary encounters, engaging with the parents in a "cycle of coercion" in which parents lose their ability to control the child's behavior by other than threats and physical force (Patterson, 1986). Physical abuse is frequently precipitated by the child's antisocial behavior, defiance, fights with a sibling, or inconveniencing the parents by messing up or bedwetting

(Herrenkohl, Herrenkohl, & Egolf, 1983; Kadushin & Martin, 1991). The child's activity level, behavioral reactions, and appearance are factors that contribute to punitiveness in parents who are irritable or untrained in the use of effective disciplinary methods.

The overall rate of maltreatment known to professionals indicates that it increases with the age of the child up to mid-adolescence (National Center on Child Abuse and Neglect, 1988). This higher rate may be because adolescents are more likely than young children to report abuse to school or legal authorities, or to justify their delinquent behavior on the basis of abuse. Families of adolescents who report abuse have higher social status than families of younger children, perhaps because more middle-class than poor adolescents will bring abuse to the attention of trusted adult authorities. As discussed earlier, adolescent girls are especially susceptible to the adverse effects of their mothers' divorce and remarriage, and to sexual abuse from stepfathers. Adolescents at high risk for maltreatment appear to be less socially competent, with lower frustration tolerance and less developed social skills (Berdie & Wexler, 1984; Libby & Bybee, 1979). Since most abused adolescents report that they were also abused as children (even when their abuse as children was not reported), their externalizing problem behavior may be the result, as much as the cause, of persistent mistreatment.

Although there are positive child attributes (such as attractiveness, calmness, and docility) that may decrease the likelihood of a child being targeted for abuse, the circumstances that enable abuse to occur, more than the personal characteristics of the abuser, should be the preferred focus of prevention and intervention. The application of concepts of resilience or vulnerability to the problem of child abuse is diversionary when it implies that the focus of prevention or intervention efforts should be on adapting the victim to the abusive circumstances—that is, in promoting "invulnerability." For most abused children, even a history of secure attachment does not render the child invulnerable to the effects of parental abuse (Farber & Egeland, 1987). The very factors that are protective for children exposed to such stressors as divorce (Hetherington, Cox, & Cox,

1982) or parents' illness (Werner & Smith, 1982)—as, for example, a responsive, well-organized, structured household—are usually absent in abusive families. A child may give the appearance of being "invulnerable," but show the effects of having been abused many years later.

Summary

The locus of control for parents' abusive behavior should not be shifted to the victim. Children's attributes or conditions immediately precipitating abuse are not the main generic causes of maltreatment (Herrenkohl, Herrenkohl, & Egolf, 1983). Although the child's own behavior is the most frequent reason given by parents for physical abuse, and doubtless does contribute to parents' frustration and anger, most parents do not respond with physical abuse to their children's troublesome or provocative behavior.

There are family circumstances that increase the stress of parenthood or diminish the parent's capacity to be a competent caregiver. These circumstances include having a first child especially when very young, withdrawal of spousal support, rearing a nonbiologically related child, and having a vulnerable or defiant child. Acrimonious spousal discord deprives the primary caregiver of support, and adds directly to her (usually it is the mother) stress. Poor black women are most likely to be single and young at the birth of their first child. This combination of circumstances is highly associated with maternal distress, which in turn increases the likelihood that she will not be a competent caregiver. Social and intimate support from trusted family members may buffer the effects of adverse circumstances on the primary caregiver. Family risk factors are mutually reinforcing, and all are less likely to eventuate in child abuse if the study population is affluent. Although it may be desirable to examine each risk factor in isolation in order to determine its unique contribution, it should be recognized that this practice violates the ecological premise that the variable-in-context has an effect that it would not have were it embedded in a different context.

CHAPTER FIVE

Systems Approaches

There are a variety of overlapping systems approaches to the etiology and treatment of child maltreatment that have in common concern with multidirectional causal processes and subsystems (e.g., the spousal dyad) as they affect, and are affected by, the whole family system. Systems theorists are concerned with the etiology and treatment of psychopathology, and thus with risk factors that increase the likelihood of a negative outcome, especially in vulnerable individuals. They are also interested in sources of resilience within the individual and protective factors in the environment that promote positive child outcomes (Rutter, 1979, 1987). Systems approaches to child abuse are theoretically coherent and empirically fruitful. Because of their ambitious effort to encompass many contexts and dimensions, however, systems approaches to studying the family are sometimes flawed in execution by shared method variance and nonvalidated measures.

Theoretical constructs central to systems approaches to family functioning are risk, vulnerability, buffering, resilience, and invulnerability.

Risks are external or internal factors such as poverty, child abuse, shyness, and marital conflict that predispose identifiable groups and individuals to negative developmental outcomes such as delinquency, ill-health, and depression. Some external risk factors such as poverty or parental abuse are sufficiently toxic that they endanger the child in most areas of functioning. Other risk factors may instigate processes that result in positive as well as negative outcomes. Thus, shyness, as an internal risk factor, predisposes some children to depression, but can protect inner-city children from becoming delinquent, unless the child is not only shy but also aggressive (Kellam, Ensminger & Turner, 1977).

The other constructs central to systems approaches to family functioning—vulnerability, buffering, resilience, and invulnerability—are intended to explain why not all individuals at risk develop a disorder, and indeed why some individuals appear to thrive on the challenges that a risk status may present. In the presence of a risk, vulnerability increases, and buffers and resilience decrease the likelihood of a negative outcome. *Buffers* are factors that protect against external threats and internal vulnerabilities. *Resilience* implies that some individuals are more resourceful psychologically, skilled interpersonally, or stronger physiologically than others, so that they are able to grow hardier in response to a challenge that would cause a more vulnerable individual to regress or crumble. The term "resilience" is preferable to the term "invulnerable" because no individual is impervious to stress or catastrophe.

Because a risk factor, as the term is used by Rutter (1979, 1987) or by Masten and Garmezy (1985), can be an internal or an external instigator of a set of processes that occur over time, the distinctions between risk and outcome, or risk and vulnerability appear to depend entirely on the investigator's perspective. Thus, parental abuse may be regarded as an outcome of poverty, but also as an external instigator of internal processes in children that increase their risk for developmental abnormalities. Vulnerabilities, according to Rutter, are not independent main effects, but operate only in the presence of high-risk factors. However, since vulnerabilities and risk factors are each said to amplify the effects of the other, the designation of which factor is a risk and which is a vulnerability depends on the theoretical predilection of the researcher. *In the interests of clarity it might be advisable to reserve the terms "risk" and "buffer" for events external to the subject that respectively threaten or protect his or her welfare, and the terms "vulnerability" and "resilience" to internal processes that amplify or reduce the probability of negative outcomes when the subject is threatened by high-risk events.*

Family Systems Approach to Etiology

Family therapists who adopt a systems approach (Haley, 1976; Minuchin, 1974, 1985) recognize the importance of the larger ecosystem within which the family is embedded, but generally identify the family as the social system of most significance to the individual. Family systems therapists place the individual within the organized family system and the family within a generational cycle in the transmission of family pathology. Incest, for example, has been conceptualized as an intergenerational problem that requires treatment of the entire dysfunctional family, rather than solely of the perpetrator and victim (Alexander, 1985; Friedman, 1988; Justice & Justice, 1979). The incestuous family system is described as excessively enmeshed, with poorly defined intergenerational boundaries; its members are unable to establish clearly defined individual identities, and are unwilling to assimilate input coming from sources external to the family. The perpetrator expects to be indulged by the spouse and even by the child victim, who often assumes adult roles within the family system. Incest, however, is the product not only of individual and family pathology, but also of gender stereotypes, such as equation of sex and aggression with masculinity and of dependency and submission with femininity (Finkelhor & Lewis, 1988). Although most incest perpetrators are men, frequently stepfathers, either parent may regard a child as chattel and not recognize the fiduciary obligations that normally conscientious parents acknowledge toward their children, which bar overt expression of incestuous and other exploitative feelings.

Transactional Models

A transactional model, such as that proposed by Sameroff and Chandler (1975), focuses on the interactions between reproductive or other internal vulnerabilities and caregiving environments that determine outcomes. Low birth weight of an infant is an example of a reproductive vulnerability that interacts with low income (an environmental risk factor) to overtax the limited resources of emotionally disturbed mothers. Sameroff and Chandler cite the well-known studies of Drillien (1964) and McDonald (1964) to demonstrate that prematurity (a reproductive vulnerability) has little effect on IQ in high-income homes, but a retarding effect on IQ in low-income homes. Werner and Smith (1982) have shown that low socioeconomic status has fewer adverse effects on low birth weight infants when good prepaid prenatal and postnatal care is available to all women, as it is in Hawaii.

There is evidence that many abused children have presenting problems before they are abused (Gil, 1970; Morse, Sahler, & Friedman, 1970). Abusive parents overreact to noncompliance because they tend to perceive their children as more difficult and unmanageable than do more objective observers (Reid, Kavanaugh, & Baldwin, 1987). Because abusive parents reason at a lower level about family problems than do nonabusive comparison parents, they regard a "failure to thrive" infant as simply oppositional or stubborn. Such parents may be taught to redefine their child's cry as a signal for hunger—a higher level of reasoning—and therefore to respond more appropriately with care rather than with anger. This is an example of a "redefinition" intervention (Sameroff & Fiese, 1990), that could help parents of "difficult" children cope with them more compassionately.

Developmental/Organizational Theory

Sroufe and his colleagues (see Sroufe, 1979; Sroufe et al., 1985; Sroufe & Rutter, 1984) emphasize that an understanding of psychopathological processes in abusive families must be grounded in an understanding of normal developmental processes. Child maltreatment, for example, is expected to have different effects depending on the salient developmental issues with which it interferes. The developmental issues identified as salient up to one year of age are attachment and biological regulation; between ages one and one and one-half, as exploration and mastery using the caregiver as a secure base; from ages three to five, as the development of self-reliance, flexible self-control, and empathy; from ages six to twelve, as acquiring social understanding of equity and fairness, and developing a sense of "industry" and competence that facilitate school adjustment; and during adolescence, as acquiring flexible perspective-taking and a sense of identity, and establishing a firm basis for intimate friendships and a balance between connectedness and autonomy.

Guided by the developmental/organizational theory of Sroufe (1979), Egeland and his colleagues (Egeland & Sroufe, 1981a, 1981b; Egeland, Sroufe, & Erickson, 1983; Erickson, Egeland, & Pianta, 1989) assessed the psychological consequences of maltreatment. Their objective was to identify developmental consequences of various patterns of maltreatment (physical, sexual, verbal, neglectful) in a ten-year longitudinal study of 269 mothers who were considered to be at risk for caregiving problems because of lower socioeconomic status, youthfulness (mean age 20 and as young as 12 years of age), unmarried status (62%), and unplanned pregnancy (86%). Of these, 44 cases were identified as abusive and divided into (overlapping) focus groups—physically abusive (24), neglectful (24), hostile/rejecting (19), and psychologically unavailable (19). The contrast group from roughly the same ecological niche consisted of 65 adequate caregivers (that is, mothers not presently abusive, or regarded as likely to become abusive). All children were first-born and about the same age. Mothers were observed with their children and queried about their own upbringing to assess "generational transmission." By identifying a contrast group of adequate caregivers in a low-income population the investigators could attempt to assess the consequences of abuse over and above the effects of poverty.

By contrast with Elmer (1977), Egeland and his colleagues claimed to have found many differences in attachment patterns between abused and nonabused children by eighteen months of age that were not attributable to poverty alone. There were more similarities than differences among the maltreated focus groups of children, all of whom, compared to the nonabused group, were angry and unpopular, and had difficulty meeting task demands at school and functioning independently in school and laboratory situations. The investigators concluded that the earlier the maltreatment, the more severe the consequences. Infants of "psychologically unavailable" mothers declined dramatically in performance on the Bayley scales from nine to eighteen months of age, and continued to show more severe and varied problems than did infants from the other three maltreated groups. Some of the maltreated infants appeared competent at twelve months (and thus mistakenly could have been thought of as invulnerable), but by preschool age only four of the eighteen maltreated children (22%) who were tested appeared competent on any of the tasks, and none were competent on all the tasks. By age six, eleven children had been sexually abused. The investigators conjectured that maternal insensitivity and lack of support resulted in the failure of most of the abused and neglected children to develop trust as infants, autonomy as toddlers, and conscience and industry as early school-age children. The children who experienced physical abuse were inclined to be aggressive and noncompliant, and those who experienced sexual abuse were overly dependent on adults. The negative effects of psychological unavailability and neglect were greater than those of physical abuse. By age six, the neglected children were the most severely disturbed. Because of the considerable overlap in the abuse groups, however, differences among them cannot be considered more than suggestive.

Developmental Psychopathology

The transactional models common to Cicchetti and other developmental psychopathologists begin with the premise that developmental processes emerge as a result of the interaction of biological processes, reinforcement, and parental socialization—disparate factors that must be considered simultaneously to achieve a proper understanding of pathological or normal developmental outcomes. Cicchetti and his colleagues have explored the premises of developmental psychopathology in a veritable outpouring of book chapters, offering cogent critiques of the theoretical and empirical work in child abuse and neglect. (For a representative sample, see Cicchetti, 1989, 1990; Cicchetti et al., 1990; Cicchetti & Rizley, 1981; Cicchetti & Sroufe, 1978.) These authors note the following deficiencies in the study of psychopathology and child abuse: absence of an accepted nosology and an adequate taxonomic system for reliably differentiating among the types of child maltreatment with regard to etiology or consequences; insufficient knowledge about how child maltreatment is generationally transmitted; reliance on a clinical psychopathological model that is nondevelopmental and nonecological; inadequate scientific data bearing on the efficacy of different therapeutic interventions; few prospective longitudinal studies; lack of valid comparison groups; and few comprehensive testable theories.

The empirical work of Cicchetti and his colleagues, as exemplified in the Harvard Child Maltreatment Project, is informed by knowledge of the deficiencies in the field, but, perhaps unavoidably, suffers from some of the same deficiencies in execution. The Harvard Child Maltreatment Project, a three-year longitudinal study (Aber et al., 1989), was initiated to study the etiology, transmission, and sequelae of child maltreatment from a developmental psychopathological perspective. The important questions asked included the following: Are there different types of child maltreatment with different etiologies and patterns of cross-generational transmission? How does transmission across generations occur and how can it be broken? What factors buffer children from the deleterious effects of maltreatment and what makes them more vulnerable? What are the developmental consequences of early maladaption? These questions were addressed by three studies.

The first study comprised a cohort of 190 preschool and early school-age children. Ninety-three maltreated children were compared with 67 nonmaltreated AFDC children and 30 middle-class volunteers. Interview data were collected from the parents, and structured observational data were obtained for the children. The two child factors that emerged were secure readiness to learn and to explore in the company of unfamiliar adults; and compliant, externally oriented attitudes or "outer-directedness." On the first factor maltreated children scored lowest, and middle-class children scored highest; on the second factor no significant differences emerged.

In the second study, the Achenbach and Edelbrook Child Behavior Checklist was added to the measures that had been used in the first study. There were few unique symptoms identified in the group of maltreated poor preschool children because the children in the comparison group were equally symptomatic. Mothers of school-age maltreated children, however, when compared to mothers from other groups, were more likely to report that their children were depressed and withdrawn.

In the third study, a home visit was paid to thirty-seven maltreated children and fifty-three comparison families, and the children were rated on the Block and Block Child Rearing Practices Q-sort and the Moos and Moos Family Environment Scale. Maltreated children whose parents reported encouraging autonomy less scored lower on a measure of relative cognitive maturity. Children whose parents reported enjoying them less (whether or not they were maltreated) and having less access to community resources were described by their parents as more symptomatic.

The Harvard Child Maltreatment Project was able to demonstrate that poor parents who maltreat their children, compared to those who do not, perceive their children less favorably and feel less able to tap into community resources. The effects of maltreatment on children were interpreted as "organizational" in that, from the developmental perspective of the investigators, the maltreated children were less securely attached and not as ready to engage in the challenges that school would present. The empirical findings were rather meager, however, despite the use of ecological and organizational terminology and a developmental psychopathological perspective. The study is indebted to attachment theory and methods, but otherwise is theoretically eclectic so that the putative unique advantages of the developmental psychopathological paradigm as applied to child abuse are not convincingly demonstrated.

Summary

As the work of Richard Lerner (1991; Afterword to this book) exemplifies, developmental contextualism is a view of human development that integrates life transformations of individuals with features of their historical, cultural and social contexts, emphasizing the need to conduct research in natural settings. Systems approaches to family process research employ a developmental contextualist framework. Systems approaches emphasize and attempt to study the complex interaction of personal, societal, and cultural forces in the origins of child maltreatment. They stress the importance of examining more about the transactions between the child at different stages of his or her development and the ecology or social environment in which that development occurs.

Systems approaches to understanding the etiology of child abuse situate the perpetrator within his or her family of origin and current family, and the family system within the sur-rounding ecosystem. Because systems approaches are theo-retically driven, rather than merely fishing expeditions, they are likely to use (roughly) matched comparison groups. Transactional models focus on the interactions between such child vulnerability factors as low birth weight and such environmental risk factors as poverty, which influence the level of stress experienced by caregivers that may predispose them to abuse their children. Developmental organizational theories attempt to ground their understanding of psychopathological processes in an understanding of normal development by taking into account the successive developmental tasks that are likely to be affected by abusive caregiving at each stage. In addition to these methodological advantages, systems theories, by assessing multiple domains, attempt to preserve the integrity of the ecological context in which the family functions.

Among the plethora of measures used by system theorists to assess a multitude of constructs many are not well validated. In addition, shared method variance is often not guarded against sufficiently. Thus, when information about an adolescent, his parents, and his peers are obtained from the adolescent's self-reports, the appearance of assessing multiple domains is belied by reliance on a single source. The shared method variance may spuriously inflate relations between adolescent outcomes and parenting or peer variables because of the adolescent respondent's global response tendencies to paint a picture of a happy life or, conversely, of pervasive angst. Similarly, there can be no conceptual advantage to referring to the family as a "microsystem" and access to community resources as a "mesosystem" when data on both the "micro" and "meso" systems come from the same informant.

In the absence of well-developed alternative analytic strategies, systems theorists are often forced to resort to traditional path analytic or multiple regression methods that take a variable (such as mother's age) out of context in order to examine its effects. The whole language of independent, dependent, and mediating or moderating variables, however, contradicts the main tenets of systems theories that purport to examine the operation of a system as a whole. Systems research strategies are not congruent with reliance on current research strategies that examine the unique or additive (rather than interactive) effects of causal variables on child outcomes. Parceling out variation into its likely causes to determine the "unique" effect of a variable belies the underlying maxim of systems theories that the effect on an outcome variable of any one variable (e.g., of mother's age on incidence of abuse) depends on the total context of variables (e.g., socioeconomic status and family structure) in which that variable is embedded.

Granted that in human development everything interacts with everything else, we still need to know how specific developmental processes interact with specific environmental forces to affect specific child outcomes. If the researcher who embraces a system's theory resorts to a data analytic strategy that makes use of partial correlations in multiple regression or path analyses to evaluate the "unique" effect of a causal event, that integrity is compromised in practice no less than by the more traditional unidirectional studies that systems theorists critique. These more traditional studies of parent-to-child effects will be discussed in chapter 6.

CHAPTER SIX

Childrearing Dimensions Relevant to Child Maltreatment

According to Scarr (1992), "Ordinary differences between families have little effect on children's development, unless the family is outside of a normal, developmental range" (p. 15). Although I contend that Scarr is not correct when she asserts that variations within normal families are unimportant determinants of children's development (Baumrind, 1993), extremely abusive and neglectful parenting practices clearly fall outside the normal developmental range. Therefore, data obtained from research with nonabusive middle-class samples has unknown applicability to an understanding of frankly abusive parents from a welfare-dependent or clinic population.

Data obtained from normal families usually focus on facets of responsiveness (warmth, reciprocity, attachment) and demandingness (firm control, monitoring, positive and negative reinforcement). These two (orthogonal) factors (responsiveness and demandingness) emerged from the early analyses of Schaefer (1959) and Becker (1964), and are still considered to be the central dimensions of childrearing (Maccoby & Martin, 1983). Compared to normal families, we can expect both abusive and neglectful parents to be less responsive as well as more punitive, and neglectful parents to be less demanding as well as less responsive. Although these "hypotheses" are very nearly tautological, I am not aware of any empirical research that has evaluated their validity across a wide socioeconomic spectrum: The actual childrearing practices and attitudes of abusive parents are seldom if ever examined in depth and using a prospective design.

In the section on responsiveness, the literature on attachment will receive special attention because of its current prominence in understanding child psychopathology; in the section on demandingness, corporal punishment will receive special attention because of the controversial recommendation by some respected individuals and organizations that it be outlawed not only in schools but in the child's own home, on the presumption that spanking as a form of violence begets child abuse. In generalizing from healthy, largely middle-class families to the population of abusive families who are disproportionately poor, the sociological differences in the two populations must be borne in mind because they affect both the incidence and the causal nexus of parent-child relations.

Responsiveness

The seminal meaning of "responsiveness" comes from ethological theory and pertains to the meshing or mutual shaping of infant and caregiver behavior to achieve synchrony (Bowlby, 1969; Hinde, 1974). Responsiveness until recently was treated as equivalent to the affective warmth/hostility dimension. Currently, aspects of responsiveness other than warmth are being identified, and their distinctive features examined. At present, the manifestation of responsiveness that is receiving the most attention is not affective warmth, but attachment, although affective warmth is generally regarded as an important determinant of the quality of attachment in Western societies.

Warmth

Warmth refers to the parent's emotional expression of love that motivates high-investment parenting and brings about cohesive family relationships. The infant, after achieving object permanence, will anticipate how its caregiver is likely to respond to its behavior, and will use its repertoire of responses to induce its caregiver(s) to adjust their plans to take its needs into account. The infant can have only as much influence as its caregiver permits, and the caregiver's willingness to respond to an infant's demands is a function of the caregiver's empathy and affective warmth. Affective warmth and empathy in parents are associated with the development in children of conscience and an internalized moral orientation (Eisenberg, 1992; Hoffman, 1970b), and its absence with aggressive tendencies (Grusec & Lytton, 1988; Olweus, 1980; Parke & Slaby, 1983; Rohner, 1975).

MacDonald (1992) distinguished between warmth (reward system intended to facilitate cohesive family relationships and parental investment) and the security/separation distress system (which is based on fear). Warmth and intimacy, according to MacDonald, occur when there is opportunity to produce highly competitive offspring because of the availability of the requisite high levels of resources from the environment. When resources suffice, intimate spousal relationships and warm parent-child relationships will ensure parental investment. The security/ separation distress system, by contrast, functions to keep the child close to its caregiver in times of threat and requires the caregiver to be responsive to security issues, but not necessarily to be warm. MacDonald contended that secure attachment may not require affective warmth. He used Ainsworth's Ugandan data (1977) and LeVine's and LeVine's Kenyan data (1966) to exemplify circumstances in which parenting that is responsive to danger may result in secure attachment, in the absence of affection and warmth. (It is likely, however, that the anthropologists failed to detect culturally different expressions of warmth and affection in these African cultures.)

MacDonald argued that under certain ecological conditions parents will be unaffectionate and manifest low-investment parenting. When males cannot provide the resources needed for high-investment parenting, pair bonding and paternal investment in children are likely to be absent, and intimate relationships between parents, or between parents and children, will not be sought. Furthermore, caregivers caught in the cycle of poverty are less likely themselves to have been the recipients of high-investment parenting, and thus are more likely to be relatively insensitive to the reward value of warmth and affection.

In their analysis of the Parental Bonding Instrument, Parker, Tupling, and Brown (1979) identified two independent dimensions of bonding: (1) care and empathy, corresponding to warmth, and (2) overprotection, corresponding to intrusiveness. Empathic responsiveness acts to free the infant to explore, whereas overprotection acts to inhibit the infant from exploring. Secure attachment implies letting go for both participants, whereas overprotection occurs when a caregiver is more concerned with alleviating personal anxiety about the infant's welfare than in reassuring the infant of his or her availability. Caregivers who are able to achieve the difficult balance of being warm and empathic but not intrusive and overprotective are likely to establish a secure attachment relationship with their infants.

Warmth is not synonymous with noncontingent positive reinforcement. Affective warmth does not imply unconditional acceptance; a warm and loving parent may also be a firm disciplinarian. The view that the effects of contingent (in contrast to unconditional) approval are inhibiting and immoral was promoted in the 1960s by such articulate spokespersons in the fields of education and childrearing as Goodman (1964), Neill (1964), and Rogers (1960). Several studies that analyzed certain effects of noncontingent positive stimulation on young children (see, for example, Millar, 1972; Watson, 1971), however, found these effects to be highly consistent with those of noncontingent aversive stimulation. Thus, Baumrind found that unconditional approval was not associated with competence in preschool children (Baumrind, 1967, 1971a, 1972; Baumrind & Black, 1967). In these and other studies (Hoffman, Rosen, & Lippitt, 1960; Kagan & Moss, 1962; Rosen & D'Andrade, 1959) passive-acceptant and overprotective parental practices were associated in children of various ages with dependence and similar indices of low competence.

Of course, noncontingent aversive stimulation is likely to injure a child's self-esteem and sense of well-being more profoundly than its positive counterpart. The noncontingent reinforcement abusive parents dispense is aversive, and will include physical abuse and harsh disapproval. Persistent child misbehavior eliciting persistent parental disapproval is likely to reflect a past history of parental mismatch and lack of reciprocity. Frequent disapproval from a parent will demoralize a child unless it is balanced by contingent approval and noncontingent expressions of love and commitment.

Reciprocity

Maccoby and Martin (1983) and Parpal and Maccoby (1985) used the term "reciprocity" to refer to the extent to which caregivers take into account the wishes and feelings of the child. Maccoby and Martin distinguished conceptually between reciprocity based on willing compliance, which they saw as characteristic of harmonious (Baumrind, 1971b) as well as of authoritative families, and reciprocity based solely on expectation of contingent reinforcement or exchange. Parpal and Maccoby observed that a child whose mother willingly complied with his or her wishes was more likely to reciprocate with good-natured compliance to maternal demands. The notion of caregiver-child reciprocity also encompasses processes of synchrony or attunement in parent-infant interactions (see Martin, 1981; Tronick, Ricks, & Cohn, 1982). Reciprocity and synchronicity in the parent-child relationship may coexist in an affective atmosphere of mild-mannered warmth or one of abrasive confrontation or a mixture of both, but is unlikely to coexist with abuse or neglect.

Attachment

In Western societies securely attached infants generally have a reciprocally affectionate relationship with their caregivers, whereas avoidant infants, even when they show separation distress, in a likely effort to escape their caregivers' intrusive expressions of love, do not seek affectionate proximity with them.

The attachment pattern most relevant to the abuse literature is the recently identified "insecure-disorganized/disoriented" (D) attachment pattern. D dyads were first noted in middle-class samples as "difficult-to-classify": Forced classification into A (Avoidant), B (Secure), or C (Ambivalent) resulted in some insecure (A or C) infants being classified as secure (B). Egeland and Sroufe (1981a, 1981b) noted in their study of poor families that some abused infants were classified as secure at twelve months and later at eighteen months, but concluded that these abused infants only "mimicked" secure infants: Neither resistant nor avoidant, they nonetheless seemed anxiously attached. Crittenden (1985b, 1988), noting a similar paradoxical response of maltreated children to the Strange Situation, had classified such children as "A-C." Eventually these "difficult to classify" or "A-C" infants were classified as "D."

Main and Solomon (1986) describe the behavior of "D" infants as incoherent, disorganized, and dazed. Behavioral studies of their "D" mothers would provide invaluable information on the forms "maltreatment" takes (if indeed it is present) in this middle-class population. Main and Solomon do not claim that the 10% to 13% of their middle-class infants who were "difficult-to-classify," or "D," were maltreated, and since the investigators do not describe the behavior of the mothers we have no way of knowing whether they were in fact abusive. If maltreatment cannot be shown to exist, then caregivers of "D" infants should not be stigmatized as emotionally abusive on the sole evidence that the infants' behavior is aberrant and distressed. It is possible instead that "D" infants are biologically at-risk, and their autistic-like, ambivalent, confusing behavior generates, rather than results from, maternal ambivalence.

There is dispute about whether an infant can be securely attached to multiple caregivers. The claim that a singular attachment to the mother is necessary for secure attachment (monotropism) is not supported by some cross-cultural evidence (Tronick, Morelli, & Winn, 1987) or by the experience of the African American family, in which attachment to multiple caregivers is common (Jackson, 1993b). Indeed, if secure attachment requires the full attention of one caregiver, few children are likely to be securely attached in the future, because, by the time the child is two years of age, both parents now typically have to return to work to support their family.

Emic analyses are needed to establish the range of healthy adult-child bonding styles that human beings manifest in various cultures. An emic approach attempts to develop constructs, measures, and classifications of the phenomena under scrutiny from the perspective of the members of that culture, in contrast to an etic approach that imposes what is usually a European American perspective on other cultures in an attempt to formulate pan-cultural universals. An emic approach to attachment research may well reveal that there are classifications other than "B" that are more functional in alternative cultures that have developed under different ecological conditions. For example, in order to provide reciprocal support under difficult childrearing conditions African American families have utilized an extended family network. In that context, intimate contact with multiple caregivers may reassure a child that there will always be a responsible adult who is physically and psychologically available. A child reared by multiple caregivers in the African American cultural context may be adequately responsive to several caregivers, and demonstrate a pattern of behavior characteristic of neither the "ideal" "B" nor any of the other presumably less optimal classifications. Emic analyses of such children might yield a different attachment classification scheme altogether, as Jackson (1993b) postulates to be the case.

Demandingness

Demandingness, the second major factor that emerges from factor analytic studies of parenting, includes firm discipline and monitoring of children's behavior. Demandingness (as well as responsiveness) is a manifestation of high parental investment. Demanding parents directly confront, rather than attempt to subtly manipulate, their children and thus may invite open conflict with their children at points of disagreement. They supervise and monitor their children's activities, and have high aspirations for them.

Coerciveness

Demanding parents are not necessarily coercive, although they may be. Parents are being coercive when they typically issue superfluous commands accompanied by threats and promises, but not by reasons. When parents are being coercive they focus the child's attention on their powerful status rather than on the harmful consequences of the act that they wish to correct. Coerciveness may undermine internalization by irking the child and provoking opposition so that the child disobeys when the coercive parent is absent.

Confrontation

Lepper (1981, 1983) and Grusec (1983) assert that confrontational social control techniques deter internalization of prosocial attitudes, whereas covert influence techniques do not. Power-assertive confrontational upbringing may be associated as highly as avoidance of confrontational control techniques with prosocial behavior, however, provided that parents are supportive (Baumrind, 1971a), nonpunitive (Hoffman, 1963), authentic (they do not attempt to disguise inconsiderate and demeaning remarks to children as friendly confrontation), and sensitive (they take into account the extent to which a particular child can enjoy direct confrontation without becoming overstimulated). Parents' responsiveness may be evaluated by the extent to which their emotional expressivity when confronting a child matches the temperament and mood of the child. A normally resilient, hardy child will be pleasantly stimulated, whereas an introverted, vulnerable child will be disrupted by high emotional expressivity of the parent or the child (Goldstein & Rodnick, 1975).

Baumrind (1983a) argued that directly confronting children about their misdeeds, using both reason and power to persuade them to comply with parents' wishes, is preferable to covert techniques of control in many circumstances.

First, an explicit, forceful directive to share has been shown to increase rather than to decrease the likelihood that young children will continue to share after instructions and surveillance are discontinued (Israel & Brown, 1979), which suggests that noncoercive confrontation need not interfere with internalization. Direct, constraining instructions, rather than subtle or permissive instructions to help, have been found to increase cooperative, sharing behavior in young children (e.g., White & Burnam, 1975). Also, as Staub has shown in a series of studies (1971a, 1971b, 1975a, 1975b), parents' insistence that children take on responsibilities raises rather than lowers the level of their prosocial proclivities.

Second, as Eisenberg (1992) and Dunn (1988) document, infants show early empathic responses to the crying of another baby, and by eighteen to twenty-four months of age will attempt to comfort the baby. In their second and third years children increasingly imitate prosocial behavior, and as they get older engage in more actions based on other-oriented motives and self-aware perspective-taking. Children are often destructive when frustrated or selfishly motivated, and loving parents can discourage such undesirable behavior by modeling kindness and contingently reinforcing children's spontaneous acts of equity and compassion.

Third, some show of force is often necessary for the voice of reason to be noticed (Hoffman, 1970a, 1983). Parents who habitually use reason without power, after the child initially refuses to comply, signal to the child that they are indecisive about requiring compliance. Direct but rational confrontation encourages friendly give and take, and may enhance a healthy child's self-assertiveness and expand the child's repertoire of communication skills, without overstimulating, angering, or causing the child to tune out.

Fourth, children who are not made aware clearly that behavioral compliance is required do not learn that they are expected to internalize a norm requiring obedience to legitimate authority. Middle school-age children seek information to discern whether they are being "good" or "bad." When parents articulate explicit norms and then reinforce an act the child is already performing, the child's identity as a "good" child is confirmed.

Fifth, if a child clearly recognizes that the parent has the power to dispense and mediate rewards and punishments, the value to the child of receiving nurturance from that parent is enhanced (Homans, 1967; Rollins & Thomas, 1975). Power to reinforce not only legitimizes parental authority in a young child's mind but also makes the parent an attractive model to emulate (see Burton & Whiting's [1961] elaboration of the status-envy hypothesis). If the powerful parent both models and rewards prosocial behaviors, his or her ability to generate prosocial behavior is likely to be amplified.

Sixth, manipulative rather than confrontational parents are likely to produce manipulative children by modeling insincere behavior.

Monitoring

Monitoring and close supervision require considerable investment of parents' time and energy, as does the provision of an orderly, consistent regimen. Seldom are such favorable upbringing conditions present in an abusive home. Monitoring imposes restrictions on children, but these restrictions need not be intrusive or overly directive. Although in Baumrind's study (1989) the two variables were highly correlated, when mutually controlled, monitoring was associated positively with children's self-assertiveness; intrusiveness—the imposition by parents of stage-inappropriate restrictiveness—had a negative association with children's self-assertiveness. Patterson (1982, 1986) has been instrumental in demonstrating the deterrent effects of persistent appropriate monitoring on antisocial behavior of boys. In Patterson and Capaldi's (1991) study, ineffectual monitoring was largely a function of social disadvantage, and not of mothers' personality.

Inconsistent Discipline

The impact of noncontingent or arbitrary reinforcement on children's social development appears to be detrimental whether the noncontingent reinforcement is positive (approval) or negative (disapproval). Unconditional approval, like noncontingent rejection, may lead children to conclude that the environment is unresponsive to their behavior and that social causes and effects are not reliably related. Such beliefs about causality appear to deter children from trying harder when confronted with an obstacle to goal achievement. A pattern of inconsistent discipline and monitoring is typically employed by abusive parents. Thus, Young (1964) found that 100% of severely abusive, and 91% of moderately abusive, families disciplined inconsistently. In that study most abusive parents had no consistent expectations of their children and failed to provide them with guidelines or defined responsibilities. The negative effects on children of an inchoate, disorganized household are similar to those of the Disorganized/Disoriented ("D") attachment pattern discussed earlier.

Corporal Punishment

For most parents, corporal punishment is an acceptable form of discipline, and one they resort to on occasion (Gelles & Straus, 1988). Many professionals concerned about child abuse, however, categorically reject the use of physical punishment. Prestigious organizations such as the National Committee for Prevention of Child Abuse and the American Academy of Pediatricians have claimed that child abuse cannot be halted without prohibiting, or at least condemning, corporal punishment in the home as well as in the school. They laud Sweden as a country that has outlawed the use of corporal punishment. In defense of their proposed ban, they cite research that finds a positive association between children's aggression and their exposure to aggressive models (e.g., Bandura, 1973).

Although examination of the sparse relevant body of literature on the subject indicates that most studies report a positive association between physical punishment and child aggression, conclusions from these studies suffer from significant methodological flaws. There is a positive relation between prior child defiance and parents' recourse to corporal punishment, but children's defiance may provoke, rather than be provoked by, physical punishment. Although in some cross-sectional research, children who are punished physically are found to express more aggression to age-mates (e.g., Eron, 1982; Straus, 1983), results from other studies (e.g., Schuck, 1974) do not confirm that there is a relation between physical punishment and children's aggression. The few prospective studies that have used quantitative methods have yielded mixed results, with two (Johannesson, 1974; Sears, 1961) reporting no evidence for an association between corporal punishment and child aggression, and three (Lefkowitz et al., 1977; McCord, 1979; Singer, Singer, & Rapaczynski, 1984) finding a positive association. When considering the impact of physical punishment on children's behavior, the correlated effects of other parenting factors, such as affection and consistency, must be taken into account, as should such social confounds like low income and ethnic minority status.

The relation between corporal punishment and child aggression may well be curvilinear, with the most severely punished children among the most aggressive, but with permissive practices that eschew any kind of coercion also associated with higher aggression (Gelles, 1974). In support of this hypothesis, Lefkowitz et al. (1977) found that moderately punitive parents produced the least aggressive boys (compared to very harsh or permissive parents). In the Lefkowitz et al. (1977) study physical punishment increased aggression toward peers only in boys who did not identify with their fathers. Thus, corporal punishment administered by a normally loving parent may have very different, and much more positive, effects on the child than when administered by a cold and unresponsive parent.

In order to identify the effects of mild to moderate physical punishment on children's aggression or pathology, the subgroup of battered children should be omitted from the analyses. If clearly abusive and rejecting families are removed from the study population, and the prospective relationship between physical punishment and children's aggression disappears, then we should conclude that corporal punishment per se (that is, spankings that are not accompanied by rejection and painful or noncontingent beatings) does not cause children to become aggressive. On the other hand, the case against any use of corporal punishment by parents would be strengthened if even relatively mild physical punishment, as it is commonly resorted to in disciplinary encounters by most parents, results in the child becoming chronically aggressive or deeply resentful, or if parents who employ mild physical punishment initially then typically progress to become physically abusive.

The argument that spanking a child is a stepping-stone to physically harming that child is usually tautological: Willingness to spank must correlate with abuse because the few parents who have never yelled at or spanked their children, *by definition*, have never physically abused them. That does not mean that there is a "generative" relationship between spanking and abuse in the sense that spanking generally or necessarily produces abuse. (See Baumrind, 1983b, for a critique of the stepping-stone theory—in this instance of heroin use.) The evidence for the putative relationship between having been spanked as a child and becoming violent as an adult is also tenuous. Since almost all adults have been physically punished as children, and few are violent, it is unlikely that spanking routinely generates deviant, violent behavior in adults who have been spanked as children. The evidence cited to support the claim that having been punished physically as a child "causes" an adult to become physically abusive is based primarily on retrospective reports by adults, many of whom may be motivated to disown responsibility for their own violent behavior (see Parke & Collmer, 1975). In order to control for the prepotent and confounding associations between poverty and willingness to use corporal punishment, and between poverty and the presence of abuse, studies of the effects of middle class parents' use of corporal punishment on child outcomes, and on parents' later abusive behavior are needed (thus probing the stepping-stone or gateway hypothesis in that population).

It is probable that only certain parents, those who are hyperreactive to negative stimuli (Vasta, 1982), escalate from corporal punishment intended to discipline to battering. Harsh physical punishment occurring in the context of arbitrary, inconsistent discipline, an unstructured regimen, and a disorderly home environment can have no corrective purpose and for that reason alone is pathogenic. Parents who use physical punishment, but disapprove of its use, may resort to it impulsively and in anger rather than deliberatively to change a child's behavior (Parke & Collmer, 1975). When administered without guilt, under controlled circumstances in a measured fashion, where both parent and child are aware of the reason for its use, physical punishment is likely to deter unacceptable behavior. Corporal punishment administered in private for willful defiance rather than for childish irresponsibility, not in anger, and not to children younger than eighteen months or to teenagers, may well be effective and harmless in that it does not generate hostility, persistent dysphoria, or maladjustment. International comparisons fail to support a necessary tie between corporal punishment and physical abuse. Thus, there is no difference between the United States and Sweden in physical abuse despite Swedish laws prohibiting corporal punishment and significantly lower self-reports of its use (Gelles & Edfeldt, 1986). There exists no consensus in this country, as there appears to exist in Sweden, to outlaw corporal punishment on ethical grounds. The many religious conservatives who believe in literal translation of the (Judaic-Christian) Bible, including followers of John Wesley, the founder of Methodism, quote the Bible to support their duty to use physical discipline (from the Proverbs: "He who spares the rod hates his son, but he who loves him is diligent to discipline"; "The rod and reproof give wisdom, but a child left to himself brings shame to his mother"). By contrast, from the liberal-humanistic perspective of Gelles and Straus (1988) or Gil (1975), spanking is a form of violence that should be outlawed, as it is in Sweden. Gil, adopting a children's rights position, includes in his definition of abuse any act that would deprive a child of equal rights and liberty. Gelles and Straus forthrightly proclaimed their message by entitling their third chapter "From Spankings to Murder: Defining and Studying Intimate Violence." At present, such beliefs about the necessary connection between corporal punishment and children's aggressive styles of adaption or parents' escalation to child abuse, or societal violence are strongly held conjectures, no more supported by solid empirical evidence than their opposite belief that to spare the rod is to spoil the child.

I am sure we would all prefer family members to yell and hit each other less frequently. In a more nurturing society it is likely that parental stress levels could be reduced sufficiently to enable parents to discipline their children using noncoercive means. In a pluralistic society such as ours, however, where corporal punishment is acceptable to most parents (particularly to parents who are religious conservatives, low-income, or black), and where supportive services are inadequate, any attempt to outlaw corporal punishment in the home is likely to backfire. One unintended consequence of outlawing corporal punishment by parents in this society could well be to increase the incidence of neglect and emotional maltreatment of children by parents who believe in the use of corporal punishment and would then view their own children as adversaries (Baumrind, 1978b).

By contrast with American society Swedish society assures that a child will be wanted by free family planning and abortion services, and nurtures its children and their caregivers by providing families with generous child support, inexpensive health care, and day care provisions, whether or not mothers work. Within such a social context proscribing physical punishment may be effective, although as noted previously, physical abuse by many parents still occurs in Sweden.

Patterns of Childrearing

Variables in the responsiveness and demandingness domains have important unique effects on children's competencies. There are important reciprocal influences, however, among the variables in these two major childrearing domains (Maccoby & Martin, 1983). A high level of parental demandingness is best accepted by children when accompanied by an equally high level of responsiveness; a high level of responsiveness is more likely to generate optimal competence in children when accompanied by a developmentally appropriate high level of demandingness. Thus, for preadolescent children in my middle-class population (Baumrind, 1978a, 1989):

1. Parents who were both demanding and responsive (the engaged pattern and the authoritative prototype) compared to those who were neither, or one but not the other, were likely to produce children who were socially responsible and socially agentic.
2. Parents who were low on both dimensions (the unengaged pattern and the rejecting-neglecting prototype) were likely to have children who were either (a) low on both social responsibility and social assertiveness or (b)

low on non-gender-normed competencies (that is, social responsibility for boys and social assertiveness for girls).

3. Parents who were highly demanding but not responsive (the restrictive pattern and the authoritarian prototype) were likely to have daughters who were socially assertive and not highly socially responsible, but sons who did not differ from other boys.

4. Parents who were highly responsive but not demanding (the lenient pattern and the permissive prototype) were likely to have daughters who were not socially assertive but who were moderately socially responsible and sons who were similar to sons from authoritarian families, but who did not differ significantly from other boys.

In generalizing from my results when these same children were adolescents, I stated (1991a) that adolescents' developmental progress was held back by directive, officious, or unengaged practices and facilitated by reciprocal, balanced interactions—practices characteristic of both authoritative and democratic parents in my sample. Compared to children of authoritative and democratic parents, children of directive-authoritarian parents had more internalizing problem behaviors and were more likely to engage in heavy drug use. Adolescents of directive parents who were not authoritarian avoided drug use but were not as highly competent as adolescents from engaged patterns. These generalizations applied to both sexes, and to intact and separated families.

Socialization practices that appear authoritarian, punitive, or seductive by middle-class European American standards are used by many African American parents to prepare their adolescents to cope with the hazards of contemporary ghetto life, and are not indicative of mistreatment. Although an authoritative more than an authoritarian approach promotes instrumental competence in children from middle-class families (Baumrind, 1966, 1971a, 1978a, 1991a, 1991b), more restrictive practices are often necessary to protect children from dangerous and delinquent influences in the inner city (Baumrind, 1972). These parents' restrictive practices are not necessarily abusive; the conditions in which their children live are.

Studies have compared the authoritative style of parenting with other parenting styles (Clark, 1983; Dornbusch et al., 1987) in non-middle-class samples. In their large sample study (using self-report data obtained in questionnaire form from adolescents to assess both their own competencies and their parents' styles), Dornbusch et al. concluded that for the population as a whole, children's grades were associated negatively with both authoritarian and permissive parenting practices, and positively with authoritative practices. Prediction, however, was best among Caucasian students, and the negative effects of authoritarianism were absent for Latino men and for Asian men and women. Using a small sample ethnographic approach to the study of children's achievement in poor black families, Reginald Clark, an "insider," concluded that the authoritative style of mutual empowerment, high support, high expectations, close supervision, and respect for their child's intellectual achievement characterizes parents of high achievers, whereas authoritarian or permissive styles characterize parents of low achievers. Clark argues that processual variables take precedence over structural factors such as ethnicity or family intactness in generating competence. His processual descriptions of my parenting styles (Clark, 1983, pp. 2–3, 200) are concise and clear, and may be applied with little modification to any cultural group.

Summary

Research with normal families has shown that affective warmth (but not unconditional acceptance), reciprocity, and secure attachment—all expressions of parental responsiveness—are good for children. Similarly, careful monitoring and supervision (but not intrusiveness or restrictiveness), and consistent, firm discipline—all expressions of parental demandingness—are good for children. There is less consensus concerning the effects of direct confrontation on children, and no consensus concerning the effects of nonabusive corporal punishment (or, indeed, whether that is an oxymoron). The position taken here is that corporal punishment, administered by parents who are immature, egocentric, and out of control, is likely to become abusive, whereas spanking, when administered deliberatively for disciplinary purposes, is not harmful to the normally resilient child, and may legitimately belong in the disciplinary repertoire of parents.

The pattern of childrearing that has been shown by almost all investigators to be associated with optimal competence in middle-class white children, and also by some investigators with poor children of color, combines high responsiveness with high demandingness—balancing what is asked of the child with what is offered to the child. This balanced style of childrearing, called "authoritative," requires a high investment of time and resources, reciprocity of rights and responsibilities in the parent-child relationship, a well-ordered regimen, and clarity of communication. It is possible, although not likely, that an authoritative parent would be abusive, but by definition an authoritative parent could not be neglectful, because this style of parenting requires a high level of investment. It is difficult to imagine how caregivers living under impoverished conditions could devote the time or energy to a child that authoritative childrearing demands without supportive relatives or friends to assist and community resources to back them up. The levels of responsiveness and demandingness associated with the authoritative pattern of childrearing are likely to benefit any child, and thus (given biological intactness) to be sufficient to generate a healthy, competent child. This or any other childrearing style, however, is not necessary to produce such a favorable outcome. Indeed, alternative conditions of life may call for a more restrictive-authoritarian style of childrearing; and a compliant, vulnerable child might thrive better with a balance that favors responsiveness over demandingness.

The extent to which principles derived from research with normal, reasonably affluent families can be generalized to maladjusted or poor families, who are more apt to abuse or neglect their children, has not been evaluated empirically. For example, attachment classification "B," signifying secure attachment, may be beneficial to all children, and the attachment classification "D," signifying disoriented, disorganized attachment, may be harmful to all children, but so-called insecure resistant and avoidant attachment patterns may be functionally useful to children forced to cope with dangerous, deprived environments. Similarly, authoritarian-restrictive childrearing practices may provoke children to display the aggressive reactions needed to survive in the inner city, but generate complimentary submission to an aggressive parent in a physically secure environment. Thus, parent-child relations reliably established to exist in one ecological niche may not generalize to another.

There are few, if any, comparative studies that have examined cultural variations in normative parenting objectives, values, and styles, or in dysfunctional parenting patterns, using intensive observational and interview procedures and an emic perspective. The lack of such data-intensive and methodologically rigorous comparative analysis of risk factors for families in diverse social, ethnic, and cultural groups remains a critical gap in the literature on normative childrearing in the general population and on the etiology of child maltreatment.

CHAPTER SEVEN

Psychological Characteristics of Abusive Parents

Psychiatric Model

In the 1950s and 1960s the psychiatric view of the etiology of child abuse prevailed (e.g., Cochrane, 1965; Miller, 1959; Woolley & Evans, 1955), but by the 1970s there was consensus that only a minority of abusive parents were psychotic or severely depressed (Blumberg, 1974; Kempe, 1973; Parke & Collmer, 1975; Spinetta & Rigler, 1972).

Severely depressed or psychotic parents pose a developmental risk to their children, even when they are not overtly abusive. Depressed mothers tend to neglect their children, run a chaotic and disorganized household, yell and hit more, use reasoning less, and require excessive involvement in household maintenance from their children, often reversing roles with them (Crnic & Greenberg, 1987; Patterson, 1986). Severely depressed mothers are often found to provide a disruptive, hostile home environment, be only moderately involved in their children's lives, and experience friction and difficulty in communicating with other family members (Orraschel, Weissman, & Kidd, 1980; Sameroff, Barocas, & Seifer, 1984). Children of depressed parents have been found to manifest more problem behaviors than children of normal parents (Billings & Moos, 1983; Patterson & Capaldi, 1991; Radke-Yarrow et al., 1985). The associated confounds of shared genetic inheritance and social context, however, introduce ambiguity in interpretation of the relation between maternal depression and child problem behaviors, and, as Patterson (1980) has observed, children's problem behavior is often a cause, as well as a result, of caregivers' feelings of depression and low self-esteem.

Psychological Characteristics

The role of psychological factors as uniquely causal in child abuse remains ambiguous because most of the studies to be summarized did not use contrast groups, control for demographic confounds, or otherwise attempt to untangle causes and effects. Abuse may occur when a parent predisposed by psychological factors to react violently, and stressed by daily hassles, becomes overaroused by a child's misbehavior so that an initial attempt to discipline the child escalates into an act of retributive violence. Within a context of environmental risk factors, certain personality characteristics are thought to play a significant role in child abuse. Just as people predisposed by temperament or circumstances to abuse alcohol should eschew alcohol, so parents predisposed to overreact to frustration should refrain from hitting and yelling at their children.

Abusive parents are thought to share a constellation of psychological attributes that prevent them from bonding with, and nurturing, their infant (Lamb & Easterbrooks, 1981). These attributes include psychological deficiencies in empathy, sensitivity, and role-taking. Newberger (1980) posits an underlying egocentricity that prevents abusive mothers from perceiving their child as a separate individual with developmentally appropriate needs that caregivers are obligated to meet. Hyperreactivity to negative stimuli, such as an infant's crying, may predispose a parent to greater irritability or emotional distancing in response to crying (Youngblade & Belsky, 1989). There is agreement in the literature that poor impulse control characterizes abusive parents (Kempe et al., 1962; Melnick & Hurley, 1969; Steele & Pollock, 1968). Traits in the adult such as inability to tolerate ambiguity, self-centeredness, and inflexibility result in unwillingness to monitor the infant's state and signals and to provide the appropriate responses, and detract from the caregiver's ability to assess and evaluate accurately new situations. Low self-esteem and low ego-strength are said to characterize physical child abusers (Friedrich & Wheeler, 1982; Milner, 1988). As in the Melnick and Hurley study of a small sample of lower-class black abusive mothers, perpetrators generally have lower self-esteem and a higher frustration of their own need for dependence. The adult's perceived inefficacy, a function of skill as well as of the infant's temperament, affects responsiveness because the parent who feels inefficacious is motivated to disengage from interaction. External locus of control, a characteristic of children who have been abused and rejected (Phares, 1976), is said to also characterize abusive parents (Ellis & Milner, 1981), enabling many physically abusive caregivers to simply deny that they are responsible for their children's injuries (Rivara, Kamitsuka, & Quan, 1988). Parents whose causal attributions about successful childrearing outcomes are external (due to luck, societal conditions, etc.) rather than internal (due to parents' own practices and abilities) are more likely to react negatively to their child's aversive or unresponsive behavior (Bugental & Sherman, 1984).

Egeland and Erickson (1987) describe psychologically unavailable caregivers as unresponsive, detached, depressed, and uninvolved, displaying no pleasure in interaction, and failing to comfort their children in times of distress. Similar characteristics, especially immaturity, lack of empathy, low self-esteem, and self-centeredness, as discussed earlier, are descriptors often applied to the mothers of "D" infants and also attributed to adult perpetrators of incest (Justice & Justice, 1979), suggesting that such caregivers may have had parents who were psychologically unavailable. Egeland and Sroufe (1981a) found that maternal psychological unavailability or depression, rather than physical abuse, was associated with the avoidant pattern in an infant: At eighteen months, 86% of children with psychologically unavailable mothers were avoidant, with the remainder classified as resistant. Thus, any contact, even hostile contact, with caregivers harms children less than emotional withdrawal.

Intergenerational Transmission of Abuse

It is widely believed that the most important predictor of mal-treatment by a parent is abuse of that parent (e.g., Egeland, 1988; Steele & Pollock, 1968). Abuse of parents by their own parents, especially by their mothers, is an important risk factor when environmental stressors associated with poverty are present. Egeland (1988) found that of forty-seven low-income, young, single women who reported that they had been abused as children, 34% were currently maltreating their own children, and an additional 30% were in the borderline caretaking group. Since only 52% of these high-risk (that is, low-income, young, single) mothers in their study who grew up in homes where there was no evidence of maltreatment were providing adequate care, risk factors other than intergenerational transmission of abuse must have contributed to their poor caregiving practices. It is of interest that in this high-risk sample more mothers who did not report that they had been maltreated as children provided adequate care to their daughters (72%) than to their sons (37%).

The intergenerational hypothesis is controversial because it is limited by methodological difficulties of definition, reliance on reports of offenders already labeled as abusive, and supported primarily by retrospective designs. Kaufman and Zigler (1987) argue that studies affirming the intergenerational transmission hypothesis are flawed by absence of control groups, biased retrospective self-report, and the subjectivity of the case study approach. Bias is introduced when parents cited for abuse seek to disown responsibility for their behavior by blaming their own parents. Adults who were abused as children but are not themselves abusive may underreport in an effort to save their family of origin embarrassment, or because they feel that they deserved the punishment they received. If, as seems likely, relative to each other, abusive parents are more likely to overreport, and nonabusive parents to underreport having been abused by their own parents, response bias would provide spurious support for the intergenerational hypothesis. The prospective study of Egeland and his colleagues that is not based on retrospective accounts and case studies, however, also supports the intergenerational hypothesis. Since one-third of abused parents admit to abusing their own children, and more may inflict abuse subsequent to having been studied, sufficient evidence exists to infer that intergenerational transmission is one important cause of abuse. What, then, is transmitted and by what processes?

Four processes whereby harsh (not necessarily abusive) parenting might be transmitted across generations were proposed and then tested by Simons et al. (1991) using structural modeling techniques. They found evidence for a direct modeling effect from grandparent to parent, resulting in reflexive recourse to use of physical punishment. They found (surprisingly) no evidence for the social class hypothesis that adult children inherit the social class of their parents with its accompanying stresses and lifestyles. They found (weak) evidence that harsh parenting fosters hostile personalities in parents, resulting in harsh treatment of their children, and that a philosophy favoring harsh discipline is transmitted across generations. They concluded that the process of intergenerational transmission of abuse takes place through modeling, and by impairing the ability of an abused child to develop empathy and adequate impulse control, or trust in oneself or others.

The most frequent explanation of intergenerational transmission of maltreatment, when it does occur, comes from attachment theory: The child who is abused at an early age constructs an internal working model that best fits the reality experienced by the child when young. That internal working model is resistant to contrary experiences that occur when the child gets older, and in turn influences the way such individuals will respond to their own children by increasing the likelihood of abuse (Main & Goldwyn, 1984). According to Crittenden (1985a, 1988), abusive mothers behave as though they perceive the world from an adversarial perspective, requiring that they maintain sole control; neglectful mothers behave as though no one cares enough to meet their needs, resulting in protective withdrawal.

If an individual who was abused has certain experiences subsequently his or her representational model can be positively altered. Mothers able to break the cycle of abuse are more likely to have received support from a nonabusive adult as a child;

have been in therapy; have a supportive, satisfying current relationship with a mate; have less life stress and be psychologically healthy (Egeland, Jacobvitz, & Sroufe, 1988). Some investigators (Belsky, Youngblade, & Pensky, 1990; Elder Nguyen, & Caspi, 1985) offer evidence that the physical attractiveness of abused women who are able to break the cycle of abuse has drawn supportive partners to them. Many abused mothers do in fact establish healthy relationships with a partner as adults (Egeland, 1988). There are few clues in the literature, however, to indicate what characteristics of the individual (other than physical attractiveness) or circumstances (other than affluence) could allow such a fortuitous bond to be established, so that the victim's representational model of the self as unworthy of love, and others as inadequate or abusive care- givers, could be so radically altered.

Prospective studies are needed that examine factors related to breaking the cycle of abuse in maltreated children who do not maltreat their own children. It is also necessary to examine the processes and mechanisms that result in mal- treatment by parents who have not themselves been maltreated.

Summary

It is generally acknowledged today that few abusive parents are severely or chronically disturbed. A constellation of personality traits frequently found to characterize abusive parents includes deficits in empathy and role-taking, poor impulse control, low self-esteem, and an external locus of control. Abuse by one's own parents is neither a necessary nor a sufficient condition for abusing one's own children. About one-third of abusive parents, however, do claim that they were abused as children.

Breaking the cycle of abuse requires integration of negative childhood experiences into more positive working models of relationship. Changed circumstances, such as in- creased material resources, and physical attributes of formerly abused caregivers that draw supportive partners to them are factors that have been found to enable many women to break the cycle of abuse. The most consistent protective factors appear to be emotionally supportive experiences with a loving caregiver in childhood and adulthood. For many, however, breaking the cycle of child abuse requires breaking the cycle of poverty. Simons et al. (1991) not withstanding, intergenerational transmission of abuse may be an artifact of intergenerational transmission of poverty or affluence.

CHAPTER EIGHT

Recommendations

Research on Family Life

Unless and until there is social consensus among parents or professionals about what constitutes child maltreatment there can be no accurate estimate of its incidence. A much better understanding of the way class and culture shape parents' childrearing goals and practices is needed in order to formulate (relatively) invariant, unambiguous, and conceptually clear theories of child maltreatment. Studies of the forms that maltreatment takes in the middle class where the confound of poverty is not present, and of optimal parenting as it occurs in a social context of minority status and poverty, are requisite.

Research questions that should be asked include the following:

- What characterizes parents who are good caregivers, although "at-risk" in that they are impoverished, have been abused, are under twenty, or are subject to a high level of environmental stressors and hassles?
- What is the prevalence of middle-class abuse, and what are its unique manifestations, if any?
- How do the manifestations of abuse and neglect vary across disparate ethnic and income groups?
- How does the hopelessness and helplessness of the chronically impoverished affect their expectations for their children and the investment they are willing to make in them?

- How does substance abuse uniquely affect the incidence and manifestations of child abuse and neglect?
- Are there qualitative differences, along such dimensions as warmth, control, supervision, communication, and maturity demands, in the effects on children of optimal versus acceptable, or minimal versus substandard versus abusive practices?
- To what extent are standards of optimal, acceptable, minimally acceptable, substandard, and abusive care universal or culturally diverse?
- How do parents from various American subcultures learn to nurture their children, and how can educational programs for parents be adapted to accommodate culturally diverse values and needs?
- How acceptable to non-middle-class parents are suggestions that they should reason with children rather than issue unelaborated directives?
- To what extent is there a generative causal link between corporal punishment and abuse? When caregivers are proscribed from the use of corporal punishment, as they are in Sweden, do they then tend to become psychologically unavailable?
- How can alternatives to corporal punishment be made acceptable to social groups that value its use? Is "time-out" in fact perceived as an effective alternative to corporal punishment by members of such groups?
- Are there unique effects on children of verbal abuse, and are parents conscious of these effects?
- What are the differential effects on children at different stages of their development of the various parental practices grouped under maltreatment?
- Are cognitive levels of reasoning about parent-child problems associated with differential quality of caregiving?

Evaluation of the effects of ameliorative social programs on child abuse and neglect requires random assignment between contrast programs; use of high-quality measures; experimenters and coders blind to the abusive status of subjects; evaluation by objective, nonprogram personnel; and broadening the ecological niches that are sampled to include nonpoor parents.

Prevention/Intervention

The position taken in this book is that the generative causes and cures of legally actionable child abuse and neglect are primarily social-structural rather than psychological. Belsky (1991) goes so far as to assert that given the harsh realities of their life even maltreatment (very low involvement parenting) is adaptive for impoverished ghetto families. That is, when resources are insufficient to meet the basic needs of the family, it may be necessary for parents to selectively neglect or ignore the needs of some of their offspring, so that other better fit family members may survive. To the extent that Belsky is correct we have a definition of an abusive society—one that impels parents to be harsh and neglectful to some of their children so that others may physically survive to reach biological maturity. We need to understand why the majority of parents living under impoverished conditions do not abuse or neglect their children, and how some remarkable parents are able to buffer the effects of poverty and prejudice on their children, and to rear competent, successful adults against such odds.

A federal commitment to children's welfare equivalent to that accorded the elderly is required to break the cycle of child poverty. More is already known about the "forgotten half" of our society than is being utilized to alleviate the social conditions that contribute directly to poor child outcomes, and indirectly to helplessness and hopelessness in caregivers so as to predispose them to neglect or abuse their children. The ability of parents to provide a healthy childrearing environment is severely constrained by poverty, and what parents do or fail to do affects child outcomes in crucial ways. The greatest threat to poor children's welfare is society's neglect (American Humane Society, 1983), not their parents' neglect or abuse. Battering, sexual abuse, and psychological mistreatment, serious as they are, are not as worthy of public outrage as the social policies in the United States that have contributed to neglect of the welfare of children and their mothers, especially in inner-city nonwhite communities, where homelessness, grinding poverty, racism, poor health care, untreated substance abuse in women of childbearing age, adolescent prostitution, and children having children all persist.

At the minimum a child abuse prevention network should provide:

- affordable contraceptive services to prevent conception of unwanted children
- culturally sensitive classes in parenting for high school youth and other parents-to-be
- prenatal care and counsel to all mothers at risk
- leave for parents during the immediate postnatal period
- educational and home visitor support services for all primipara
- prompt and regular well-baby medical care for all children
- quality child-care facilities at reasonable cost for all families
- outreach child and family services to homeless families
- treatment programs for abused and neglected children and their parents
- financial and emotional support for indigenous caregivers within a community to facilitate effective functioning of such informal caregiving networks as may already exist

Prevention programs that violate parental standards, or health workers who are seen as disapproving and officious, tend to be ineffective (Crockenberg, 1987). Thus, among fifteen programs studied in California, parent meetings were attended by only 13% of those with children in first to third grades, and by 34% of parents with children in preschool programs (Gilbert et al., 1989). Apparently, the majority of parents for whom the programs were intended did not find them helpful. Effective long-range programs of intervention are very costly, but as Weber, Foster, and Weikart (1978) have shown, they are in the long run cost-effective.

Broad prevention programs with health care and home visitor components that build on the strengths of families, thus empowering parents, and that offer parents training in nonabusive forms of discipline, seem to have been the most effective of the early childhood intervention programs (Lazar et al., 1977; Zigler, Taussig, & Black, 1992). There are effective programs (e.g., Whiteman, Fanshel, & Grundy, 1987) that show parents how to use such methods of discipline as "time-out" or inductive reasoning together with verbal disapproval as alternatives to corporal punishment. The Perry Preschool Project (Barnett & Escobar, 1990; Weber, Foster, & Weikart, 1978), the Syracuse University Family Development Research Program (Lally, Mangione, & Honig, 1988), the Yale Child Welfare Research Program (Seitz, Rosenbaum, & Apfel, 1985), and the University of Rochester Nurse Home-Visitation Program (Olds, 1988) all have reported long-term positive effects of their ongoing home visitor programs on family functioning, with the University of Rochester program said to reduce verified child abuse and neglect among poor, unmarried teenagers.

If the worth of a society should be judged by the concern of one generation for the next, ours has been found wanting. We in the United States neglect our children, middle-class or poor. In analyzing the conditions that generate maltreatment by parents of children, I have focused on the families of the poor because this is the stratum of society that has been the most victimized. The contact parents have with their children in all strata of society in the United States today has decreased drastically, however, and this greatly reduced contact should itself be regarded as a form of neglect. Low-investment parenting is becoming the norm rather than the exception, as both parents, from necessity or choice, leave their children, at ever-younger ages, in the care of poorly trained and poorly paid attendants. Young children require personal care from reliable adults to whom they are attached, and who devote the sustained attention and time needed to facilitate their sensory-motor development as infants, and their language, social, and moral development throughout early childhood. I know from personal experience, and from observation of successful parents in my longitudinal study, that difficult as it may be, it is possible for adults in middle-class, two-parent families to stagger their work schedules so that they are able to spend many daytime hours with their young children, and to have the time to properly train and supervise their surrogates when the parents themselves must be absent from the home.

Parents need all the help they can get from a caring community. Children's participation during part of the day in infant and preschool programs may be advantageous, provided that the child care staff is stable, well paid, well trained, and dedicated to furthering the development of each child. For single parents or poor families such infant and child centers are essential adjuncts that can reduce the stress felt by isolated parents, enable them to go out of the home to work, and teach them, when desired, more supportive and mutually rewarding patterns of interaction with their infants and young children.

In Sweden anyone with a child under eight years of age may work a six-hour day; parents are enabled and encouraged to stagger their work shifts; and high-quality infant care and preschool programs are provided to promote children's well-being, character, and competence. We in the United States are obligated to provide our families with at least a fraction of the benefits that Sweden and many other European countries offer their citizens. It is still the responsibility of adults to choose if and when they will have children, and then to commit themselves fully for at least two decades to nurturing and guiding those children. Every child is entitled to be brought up by responsible parents who in turn are fully supported by a responsive community.

Hit by Friendly Fire: Iatrogenic Effects of Misguided Social Policy Interventions on African American Families

Jacquelyne Faye Jackson

I have read your manuscript and I want to congratulate you on a truly stellar, incisive piece. You have correctly identified society and features of its social structure as probable prime causes of child maltreatment. This contrasts with the view of many psychologists, who attribute primary blame to intrinsic traits of abusing caregivers not to pernicious effects of the society's structure that are actualized in the intimate environment of caregiver-child relations. Your approach comports with the issues I raised in my recent *Child Development* article (Jackson, 1993a) critically responding to Sandra Scarr, which focused on the currency of genetic determinist explanations for complex, problematic social behaviors.

I would like to address, however, some important omissions in your study. You commendably identified prejudice and poverty as contributing factors in general, but did not delineate their social-institutional expressions that contribute to the incidence of child maltreatment. Having identified social-structural features of this country as primary causes in the escalation of child maltreatment, I think that it is important to include a discussion of specific public policies and social intervention practices that coercively predispose parents and family caregivers to become abusers. Specifically, I have in mind policies of

the post-World War II era including those that disproportionately affect African Americans. I think a recent historical
perspective is needed because of the current emphasis on
intergenerational transmission of abuse, and I think explicit
attention to race is required because of the unstated focus of the
maltreatment movement on African Americans in spite of
disclaimers to the contrary. To give you some idea of what I have
in mind, I will use rhetorical questions to discuss briefly a select
few of the numerous overlooked issues that need urgent
attention.

- I. Single-parent household status is a major risk factor
  for child maltreatment, and in the United States it is
  most prevalent among African Americans. What caused
  the explosion of single-parent households since World
  War II?

Poverty per se does not account for the incidence of single-
parent households among African Americans or other groups.
During historical periods of greater poverty than any since
World War II, single-parent households were far less prevalent
among African Americans and other groups than they have
become. I maintain that discriminatory exclusion from the work
force starting with the recessions of the late 1940s and 1950s
coupled with the prohibition of welfare support to two-parent
families from the 1930s to 1988 created the ignominious, poor,
single-parent African American family and contributed to the
rise in single-parent families in general.

In all states prior to the 1970s and in most up until the
1980s, as a matter of federal or state policy, welfare support
to families with dependent children (AFDC/ADC) was restricted
to mothers without husbands or adult male partners living in the
home. Moreover, this rule was enforced on a selective, discriminatory basis with surprise night searches for males in the
homes of African American women who received AFDC,
discriminatory expulsion from the AFDC program of African
American women found to have had cohabiting male partners,
selective pressure on African American women to divulge the
whereabouts of the fathers of their children for purposes of
disqualifying the mother and child for receipt of AFDC whether

or not the fathers were capable of replacing the lost income, and selective pursuit of biological fathers of African American child recipients of AFDC for child support payments in lieu of, but not as a supplement to, welfare payments. These policies created a "marriage handicap" that literally tore African American men from their families. Along with the discriminatory employment climate of the recessions of the 1950s, 1970s, and 1980s, and the disproportionate military conscription of African American males in the 1960s, these welfare policies imposed obstacles to marriage over several generations that were almost as insurmountable as the legal prohibitions against marriages of African Americans during slavery.

These welfare policies directly contributed and continue to contribute to the incidence of severe child punishment and abuse in ways that are not acknowledged in the social science literature. I have never seen a discussion of the fact that children are often used as naive and unwitting informants in investigations to detect the inhabitants of a household or its frequent visitors. Children were frequently interviewed by visiting social workers, teachers, and inquiring detectives presenting themselves as curious strangers about the whereabouts of male figures in their lives. Child disclosures that lead to or threatened to lead to information on maternal partners—and therefore seriously threatened the family income—precipitated severe and ostensibly irrational punishment of the child by either or both parent figures. Moreover, the threat of an economic crisis brought on by child disclosure of a maternal partner is a current issue in spite of the liberalization of the laws on receipt of welfare by two-parent families. Unemployed men who live with their families will soon be obliged to work for a portion of the welfare benefits the family receives. Since the welfare stipends are uniformly well below a viable family income, men who secretly live with their families and make a financial contribution that *supplements* the welfare stipend clearly will contribute more than the "workfare" fathers; this perpetuates the institutionalized coercive pressures toward duplicity that have always been a part of involvement in the welfare system. It also challenges parents to explain their duplicity to their children in ways that will ensure children's disinclination to unauthorized disclosures, and it predisposes disclosing children to parental punishment that may be as severe as abuse.

- II. Why do so many African Americans, particularly those of low income, condone corporal punishment and appear to engage in child punishment without reasoning?

Coerced duplicity is a determining factor for both welfare recipients and nonwelfare working parents. The circumstances and dilemmas of welfare mothers, however, are the most dramatic. In addition to keeping secrets about males who may be members of the household, many welfare recipients have been forced to keep secret information about other sources of supplement to their AFDC payments as well. Moreover, explaining maternal maneuvers growing out of grappling with the need for secrecy to enlist the compliance and assistance of children is proscribed by the constraints of children's cognitive immaturity as well as by mothers' moral ambivalence about such coerced survival strategies. These latter factors stymie maternal reasoning with children.

Since the inception of the welfare system, many welfare recipients have worked to supplement their AFDC payments. They have been employed at menial domestic, janitorial, and child care jobs in the cash economy where prevailing standards counter reporting wages for payroll tax purposes. Some also earn money in the underground economy of marginally legal or outright illegal enterprise. Parents who are struggling for survival under such circumstances feel pressure to carefully control information about themselves because of the real possibility that disclosure of their work activities might lead to loss of welfare benefits, prosecution for welfare fraud, or prosecution for other offenses. In order to counter the threat that talkative, naive children will divulge family secrets regarding maternal livelihood, many welfare mothers are coerced to use disciplinary tactics that make their directives salient in their children's experience.

Working parents without involvement in the welfare system have been coerced into duplicity as well. After severe cutbacks in the public-sponsored child care provided during the

World War II era boom in work opportunities that drew most African Americans out of the south and into the north, there has always been a shortage of child care for working African American women. In addition, many working African American women, even those from relatively high socioeconomic backgrounds, have been forced to take jobs that are undesirable to majority workers—for example, jobs with night and evening hours or split shifts—in order to remain in the work force. Usually such jobs created child care problems because of the shortage of child care providers who would accommodate working mothers with nonstandard work schedules. As a consequence, child care has been provided in many instances by marginally competent juvenile child caregivers or by televisions. Given their inability to directly supervise their children, many working women have relied on disciplinary tactics that are salient in the children's experience to increase the probability of child compliance with directives.

African American working mothers who are not welfare recipients have relied on other women who were welfare recipients as caregivers on a widespread basis. This arrangement brought the children of nonwelfare families into the sphere of those under pressure to avoid disclosure of the supplementary income derived from paid child caregiving of welfare recipients. In some instances, it also precipitated physical punishment of the child in care for reasons similar to those related to precipitation of physical punishment of disclosing children of welfare recipients.

Mothers relying on unorthodox child care without adult supervision have also run the risk of detection and prosecution by public child protection agencies. In cases where accidents occurred and the unorthodox child care arrangements came to the attention of the authorities, mothers were not only charged with the criminal offense of child neglect and endangerment, but had their children taken from them and placed outside their homes in foster care. Provision of appropriate child care in lieu of prosecution and removal of children from the homes by intervening agencies has been rare. This fact has led many in the African American community to avoid such public agencies when in need of child care assistance, and to rely on stringent enforcement of directives to unsupervised children with unapologetic use of physical punishment.

- III. Reportedly, African Americans value and live in extended families. Why haven't their extended families been effective in stemming the tide of child maltreatment?

Extended families as well as nuclear families have been the target of family-fracturing public policies, and have lost some of their child protective capacities as a result. National and local government policies from the late 1940s to the present lead this trend.

Concurrent to widespread discrimination in private housing and government mortgage subsidies for the building of racially exclusive suburban housing, the federal government built large housing projects with many small apartment units in the inner cities to which African Americans were confined. Local governments administering the projects restricted occupation of the housing project apartments to small family units and controlled the allocation of units in ways that prevented extended family subsets from clustering within projects. A critical result was residential fragmentation of extended families. When urban renewal policies of the 1960s were implemented, the combined effects of a reduced supply of private housing in cities, family-fragmenting public housing policies, and widespread housing discrimination led to pressures that geographically dispersed extended family subunits. Overall, housing problems reduced the number of caregivers readily available to children.

Welfare policies exerted undermining pressures on extended families as well. Payments to subunits of an extended family that chose cohabitation were reduced in relation to what each subunit would receive if housed alone; in many instances qualification for receipt of welfare was canceled because the total extended family household income exceeded levels permissible for welfare recipients. Following the establishment of purported family support entitlement programs of the 1960s, policies for food stamp and medical care programs also discouraged extended family households. The net result of these policies also removed caregivers who might support and supplement maternal care from the daily home environment of children.

Social science scholarship and public-sponsored family interventions also contributed and continue to contribute to the fracturing of extended families, particularly those contending with the sensitive task of helping their childbearing youth bridge adolescence and adult responsibilities. Their undermining role gained momentum in the 1960s when professional family services to the poor became more prevalent, and has continued to the present. Within the short space of thirty years, welfare and family service agencies implemented two contradictory sets of policies in tandem that exacerbated pervasive, tense relations between pregnant teen mothers and their parents. One set encouraged teens to sever the tie to their parents, the other compels them to be tethered. Overall, these policies have had the effect of increasing the predisposition of aggravated teen parents to vent their frustrations on their young children. The proto-typical case of the adolescent mother and her child living in the home of the young mother's parents provides a case in point.

Currently, there is a big push to require teen mothers who receive welfare to live with their own parents. Many politicians have led the public to believe that this will reduce incompetent and abusive parenting by teenage mothers. This policy does not, however, accommodate teen mothers with dysfunctional relations with their parents or those effectively expelled from their parental home. Most important, it addresses neither the existence of a norm of household independence for teenage parents induced by social service and welfare practices, nor the enormous problem of reversing the inculcated expectations of both teen parents and their parents associated with this norm.

From the 1960s through the 1970s adolescent mothers who lived with their parents were frequently advised to move to independent living quarters. Those who received social casework training in the late 1960s know this pattern of advising was guided by Freudian theoretical conceptions; these concepts specified that normative adolescent development entailed separation and physical distancing from parents, and also identified prolonged connection to parents as potentially path-ogenic and maturation suppressing. Advice was also based on emerging contentions by attachment theorists that multiple primary caregivers of infants and young children impaired emotional development of the children of the adolescent mothers. Psychoanalytically derived characterizations of poor families as prone to disorganization due to excessive family enmeshment of individual members also contributed to the practice of urging subunits of extended families to "dis-enmesh." This combination of advising practices and the concomitant growth in the number of adolescent and young adult single-mother households made a substantial contribution to the incidence of inadequate caregiving due to maternal inexperience, isolation, and depression, and to the increase of African American children at risk of child maltreatment. In other words, these practices had iatrogenic effects.

Child welfare agency practices that cause psychological schisms between children and their extended family members have become salient recently, even though they have existed for a long time. The schisms created have not only deprived children of culturally preferred sources of support, but have contributed to the risk of abuse by extended family members as well. When parental caregiving is judged inadequate by child protective agency authorities, those authorities frequently place the children involved in foster homes outside the purview of the extended family as well as the parents. Child welfare agencies frequently do not try to locate and notify extended family members of children they seize. This is currently the case in spite of federal legislation enacted in the early 1980s directing child welfare agencies to proactively engage in efforts to preserve biological families. The result is that infants and young children in the foster care system are often raised by foster parents who are geographically, culturally, and racially alien to the biological nuclear and extended families from which they came.

When children in distal foster care reach preschool or primary grade age, they are frequently returned to their biological extended families; alternatively, they are placed with African American foster parents. By that time these children not only experience the change as an emotionally disruptive crisis, but have become completely estranged emotionally from their biological families and averse to their lifestyles. In grappling with the problems of such transitions, extended family members, parents, and in some instances African American foster parents are under coercive pressure to use power-assertive disciplinary methods such as corporal punishment, which increasingly escalate to physical abuse. Moreover, relatives of transferred children, in contradistinction to foster parents, have no access to public subsidized mental health services to ease the transition. In general, biological relatives who undertake the role of primary caregiver of children with incapacitated parents get no financial or service assistance of any kind from public agencies unless they are willing to become welfare recipients.

- IV. There are a number of public-sponsored services available to low-income African Americans, such as parent education and mental health care, which are increasingly offered for the purpose of reducing child maltreatment. Why are these services frequently under-utilized?

Since the 1960s intervention services to low-income African American parents and caregivers have tapped the state of knowledge in child development for their guiding principles. That knowledge base assumed an absence of viable or worthwhile culture among African Americans, and led to a condescending aura in intervention delivery perceived as unjustified interference by many who were the targets of the intervention. Moreover, some African Americans in the community of professionals charged with the responsibility of delivering intervention programs designed by non-African Americans perceived the interventions to be detrimental. They suspected the interventions of instilling cultural disrespect and self-hatred in intervention targets who accepted the premises of the program designers. Some well-intentioned interventions spawned by the infant mental health movement provide a current example of interventions that African American professionals believe inculcate self-hatred and maladaptive behavior thus heightening the risk of infant and child maltreatment. I have reached this conclusion based on personal observations of practices in the family service professions.

I have attended conferences for practice-oriented professionals where work with African American teenage welfare recipients in Michigan based on the psychoanalytically derived theories and clinical strategies of Selma Fraiberg (1980) have been described in some detail. I have listened to these presentations closely because of my interest in cultural issues and attachment, as indicated in my recent article in *Human Development* (1993b). What I have learned is that Fraiberg's work is widely used in intervention programs for low-income African Americans in at-risk and malfunctioning mother-infant dyads. Psychoanalytically based programs constitute a crystallized form of mental health interventions with low-income African American mothers that began to emerge in the late 1960s. The Fraiberg approach involves encouraging the target mother to recall negative experiences with her own mother as a child, a procedure that Fraiberg termed ferreting out the "ghosts in the nursery." Some African American lay persons, even though they do not know or use the terminology of child development specialists, as well as some African American child development professionals including myself, fear that this ferreting out process is generating a widespread incidence of false memory syndrome and/or distorted memories.

The probability of incorrect memories is high because many of the low-income mothers in the treated infant-mother dyads were separated from their mothers and extended families during their own childhood by the intervention of child protective agencies. As a consequence, the treated mothers' knowledge of their early experiences is colored by the reports of social workers, foster parents, clinicians, and other public authorities who held substantially negative views of the functioning of the treated mothers' mothers because of the nature of their roles as public agents and the information supplied to them through institutional channels.

Currently, many child development specialists hold the opinion that mothers with negative, inchoate views of their relationships to their own mothers are disposed to poor parenting and child maltreatment, and that child maltreatment is a prevalent intergenerational phenomenon. The full set of commonplace circumstances and histories surrounding mental health interventions with low-income African American mother-infant dyads, however, lead me to fear that the identified intergenerational child maltreatment syndrome is largely institutionally induced.

In sum, I have discussed only a few of the ways in which social systems that result from public policies contribute to the incidence and escalation of child maltreatment, at least among African Americans. I urge you to bring some of the issues that I have discussed to the attention of the wide audience that will read your excellent manuscript.

Strengthening the Fabric of Child and Family Policies: Interweaving the Threads of Research

L. Annette Abrams

Introduction

Much credit is due to Dr. Baumrind for producing a conclusive review of the scholarly literature regarding race, poverty, parenting, and child abuse. Dr. Baumrind's work assists us to appreciate the multitude of variables—economic, cultural, and circumstantial—which combine in predicting a proclivity to abuse children.

As the former director of a state child welfare agency, I keenly appreciate the need for information that pulls the many threads of scholarship into a single fabric. Just as human behavior represents multiple interacting variables, so too must research reviews incorporate findings from many disciplines. Gone are the days of simplistic child protection strategies that fit neatly into the mission of a single public agency. Across the country, child and family programs are attempting to consolidate their resources and view families holistically. If research is to be usable in today's public policy arena it must be presented— like Dr. Baumrind's review—as synthetically as possible.

This commentary is intended to translate the conclusions drawn by Dr. Baumrind into public policy recommendations. It is divided into three sections:

- The first section discusses how fluctuating economic, racial, and ethnic stereotypes have historically linked America's child protection and public assistance policies. This section describes how generalizations about poor people determine the nature and degree of family scrutiny by both public assistance and child protection workers. It details the adverse impact of stigmatizing the cultural norms of nonwhite, low-income, and immigrant families. It suggests ways for child protection agencies to reduce the negative impact of applying Eurocentric, middle-class standards across all other subcultures.

- The second section discusses how the "poverty penalty" levied against poor families of color leads to alarming rates of family separation and child institutionalization, and points out the need to lift the "middle-income curtain" and enact policies that protect white, middle-class children from physical and psychological abuse.

- The third section summarizes what the scholarly literature tells us about how intergenerational poverty, job loss, and employment affect parenting and child development. This section crystallizes what the literature tells us about how to design effective parent education programs, and discusses the relationships among child care, parental employment, workplace leave policies, and proposals mandating that public assistance beneficiaries work outside the home. It also provides advice about how to assess parental needs and family circumstances more comprehensively.

How Research Can Guide Our Debate
about Child Protection: Poverty Is the
Perpetrator of Child Abuse

Dr. Baumrind convincingly identifies poverty as the single most significant predictor of child maltreatment. After years of debate based on the assumption that "abusive" parenting practices emanated from psychological flaws within the individual, her critique clarifies what weight to give poverty as a variable in the child abuse equation, and what poverty-related circumstances enhance the probability of child maltreatment.

Baumrind's conclusions have important implications for the policies, practices, and perceptions that have driven public assistance and child welfare for decades. For example, decision makers must understand the impact of stereotypes in shaping and interconnecting past public policies. Since the early years of the twentieth century, assumptions underlying child and family policy have been shaped by a combination of economic, racial, and gender caricatures. Although Aid to Families with Dependent Children (AFDC) long preceded enactment of Child Protective Services (CPS) legislation, our child welfare, social welfare, and civil rights policies too often interact with and conform to these stereotypic perceptions.

Historical Policy Connections

President Roosevelt's public jobs program, initiated during the Great Depression, exempted widows with children because of the prevailing attitude that mothers should remain in the home to care for their children. Instead of jobs, these widowed women received AFDC. In fact, the large numbers of widows and unemployed Americans during the Great Depression ennobled poverty, as opposed to prior negative stereotypes of poor people. Today's concerns about intergenerational dependence on welfare find their roots in earlier attitudes about women as single heads of households. Our biases have kept poor women in the home rather than in the workplace, forcing today's debate about economic sufficiency through welfare reform.

Nearer to the middle of the twentieth century, America came to a consensus that the children of widows deserved to grow up in "suitable" homes with two parents. Placement of poor children—especially black children—in orphanages and foster homes became a more common practice.

As policymakers reexamine policies intended to serve "the best interests" of children, they must not overlook the long-term impact of race-based stereotypes on child circumstances. The out-of-home placement patterns of yesterday have hardened in recent times. Several recent articles and studies (Hogan & Siu, 1988; Select Committee on Children, Youth, and Families, 1989; Stehno, 1982) documenting the adverse impact of race-based practices can be summarized as follows:

- Black and Latino children are more likely to be removed from their families, with Latino families undergoing more involuntary protective services intervention than other families.
- Children of color are more likely to be placed in foster care or another form of out-of-home care.
- Children of color are more likely to drift or be lost in the out-of-home system of care, once removed from their families.
- The parental rights of black and Latino parents are terminated more quickly by courts than is the case with white parents.
- Black and Latino children are less likely than their white counterparts to receive adoption services once parental rights have been terminated.
- White families receive early intervention services more frequently than their counterparts of color. Conversely, black and Latino families most frequently receive crisis services.
- Black and Latino children and families have less comprehensive service plans than their white counterparts.
- Black and Latino children are more likely to be labeled as "behaviorally disturbed" than their white counterparts.
- Professionals are less likely to stipulate mental health treatment for black and Latino youngsters. Rather,

children of color are more frequently placed in juvenile justice programs because they are seen as least likely to benefit from therapeutic services.

The 1960s and 1970s produced civil rights policies, a War on Poverty, a new definition of the role of women, and legislation to protect children from parental abuse and neglect. Dr. Jackson's commentary vividly describes how poor black families experienced a double dose of public scrutiny. Their intimate involvement with public assistance workers opened the door to judgments about the quality and acceptability of their parenting. Different racial norms collided in these low-income homes, as white social workers harshly and Eurocentrically judged black male/female relationships and parenting practices.

Authors such as Nathan Glazer and Daniel Moynihan in several publications (e.g., Glazer & Moynihan, 1965) concretized existing stereotypes about the "questionable" impact on black children of living in a female-headed, single-parent black family. The best known of these publications is referred to as the "Moynihan Report" (U.S. Dept of Labor, 1965). Many social welfare agencies concluded that low-income black family behavior was, de facto, harmful to child development and well-being. More and more, social worker visits related to the AFDC program began to trigger referrals to protective services and subsequent child removal. The pejorative picture of the black family painted by social critics was criticized vigorously by Robert B. Hill (1972) in a landmark book entitled *The Strengths of Black Families* (also see National Urban League, 1973).

Our historical tendency to stigmatize subcultures in debates about "normal" childrearing overlooks the fact that diversity is a defining characteristic of the United States. Furthermore, the complexion of our society will continue to deepen and diversify in the decades ahead. On a daily basis, social workers make culturally complex judgments when determining whether to recommend voluntary (preventive) or involuntary (legally actionable) interventions. Dr. Baumrind's examples of both optimal and less-than-optimal variations of parenting illustrate the need for child protection policy to go beyond stereotypes, and beyond black-versus-white contrasts.

Line workers investigating alleged abuse in Arab, Asian, black, Latino, or Native American households lack clear organizational guidelines regarding how to judge when parenting practices qualify as legally actionable. Not since the 1950s has our culture-at-large philosophically endorsed assimilation as a primary social objective. Nevertheless, public agencies in the 1990s continue to perform as if they expect all subcultures to personify mainstream characteristics, values, and beliefs.

Child Protection Policy Recommendations

Eight policy recommendations that follow from the preceding historical analysis are offered.

First, agencies should expose staff and administrators to a broad definition of "subculture," one that includes homelessness, poverty, race, and gender.

Second, agencies should train staff to recognize and overcome their biases in determining what is best for children from different cultures.

Third, agencies should form relationships with neighborhood-based service delivery agencies who can advise on the prevailing norms within subcultural groups, as well as within-group areas of proscribed behavior.

Fourth, when abuse is not substantiated, workers need access to culturally competent programs that will mitigate against eventual abuse.

Fifth, disciplines and professions need to focus their energy on the question of skills and inclinations, discussing which attributes and experiences incline individuals to work respectfully across cultures. Answers to this query can assist leaders in identifying staff who will be the most receptive to cross-cultural work assignments, and in offering less culturally competent staff more training or "culturally neutral" work assignments.

Sixth, standards of policy and practice should acknowledge that middle-class parents may differ from their poor black and white counterparts in at least two important ways: Middle-class parents enjoy much less agency scrutiny; and they may draw a different line on inappropriate parent-child intimacy. Dr. Baumrind notes (p. 9) that "(a)n emerging phenomenon among adult children primarily of middle-class families is public acknowledgment of 'recovered memories' of incest and child abuse that took place decades earlier." She recommends that research on the incidence of middle-class sexual and psychological abuse be conducted. Such research could clarify when non-poor children need public protection and how professionals should intervene.

Seventh, Dr. Baumrind reports that American subcultures differ on when the transfer of responsibility to children becomes unacceptable. To focus merely on the question of appropriate levels of child responsibility is to overlook the fact that current societal pressures increase the tendency for parents to "neglect" or make children responsible for themselves. One has only to review the plethora of recent "home alone" cases to understand that self-care is more than an issue of subcultural diversity in how the child's best interests are viewed. Self-care is an artifact of family life. The "home alone" or "latchkey" phenomenon is caused by lack of child care, limits on parental leave in the workplace, and parents' ignorance about their obligation to protect children.

Eighth, there is a need for clear standards of parenting and professional practice. These standards should address such questions as when, and for how long, children can be left alone without causing undesirable outcomes, and when child self-supervision constitutes legally actionable neglect.

How Research Can Guide Our Debate about Family Preservation

Agencies serving at-risk children have faced great confounds in attempting to reduce abuse, neglect, and their corollary, out-of-home placement in foster care, residential facilities, and institutions.

There has been a lack of alternatives to child removal as a response to child maltreatment. Public agencies, burdened with burgeoning allegations of abuse and neglect, deployed scarce investigative staff with only one service in their repertoire, namely, paid professional substitute caregiving outside the home of origin. In 1972 the National Association of Black Social Workers (NABSW) began to protest the disproportionate placement of black children in foster care and residential settings under prevailing child protection standards. Not until the mid-1980s did child welfare advocates have "family preservation" as an alternative to child removal. During the late 1980s the family preservation movement, seeded by philanthropic funding, spread throughout the country, with mental health agencies joining child welfare agencies in its implementation in the early 1990s.

In tandem with welfare reform came family preservation and in-home interventions as alternatives to what had heretofore been the sole response to child abuse and neglect, namely, child removal and family separation. These new interventions circumvented the "poverty penalty" by seeking funding from federal sources not tied to out-of-home care. Finally, family preservation guidelines codified a culturally responsive, assets-based approach to family functioning. For the first time, professionals were able to transcend stereotypes and to isolate poverty per se as the primary perpetrator of child maltreatment. At last, public systems could assess families holistically, calculate assets as well as weaknesses, partner with clients to define problems and identify solutions, assess the impact of cultural norms on family functioning, and have "independence from the public system" as a goal of intervention.

Until very recently, the bulk of federal/state service funds for child protection were to be used only for foster care. This funding constraint contributed to skyrocketing costs and extended lengths of stay. Relatedly, foster care funding recipients *had* to meet a poverty criterion: This "poverty penalty" preordained family separation as a consequence for those already vulnerable to public intervention and—precisely because of their poverty—at highest risk of abuse.

The result of policies predicated on a "poverty penalty" is that disproportionate numbers of children from poor families of color occupied America's foster homes for longer and longer periods of time. The "poverty penalty" began to darken the complexion of our child service system and to further confuse the relationship among poverty, race, and abuse by creating the impression that whites are less likely than others to abuse their children.

It is in this context that Dr. Baumrind's review has the greatest substance for policymakers. Dr. Baumrind's work questions the assumption that poor blacks are more likely to abuse their children. Alternatively, she suggests that blacks are no more likely to commit abusive acts but, because of the demographics of poverty *and* a lack of research on middle-class white families, the system reflexively overscrutinizes, overinvestigates, and overpenalizes poor blacks.

These conclusions are supported by what we have learned from a redefinition of child "neglect." Prior to the mid-1980s parental abuse could be substantiated solely because of a broken refrigerator, too few mattresses in bedrooms, or poor plumbing—all circumstances tied to poverty. With the advent of family preservation programs, workers were encouraged to remedy these circumstances and, when appropriate, to support caring parents in holding their families together. As a result, neglect cases linked to the artifacts of poverty plummeted in number.

Our working definitions of abuse—specifically, substantiable physical rather than psychological abuse—need to undergo a similar reframing exercise. In initiating a new look at abuse and related interventions, Dr. Baumrind suggests that the circumstances facing white middle-class children should be a focus of greater concern. She points to a recent pattern of controversial sexual abuse allegations that deserve attention. Of note as well are court cases alleging that middle-class children murdered their abusive parents, middle-class "home alone" cases, and middle-class attempts to institutionalize difficult adopted children.

As regards psychological as opposed to physical abuse, Dr. Baumrind recommends that we begin conceptualizing what forms of middle-class behavior might arguably warrant legal intervention. Her example of parents discouraging child-directed play in favor of forced academic work crystallizes policy questions that are difficult, but necessary, to deliberate.

How Research Can Guide Our Debate
about Welfare Reform
and Child Abuse Prevention

Welfare Reform

It cannot be reiterated often enough that the artifacts of poverty, rather than abusive parental practices, are transmitted across generations. We know that both poverty and affluence are transmitted from one generation to the next.

Intergenerational transmission of affluence means that each generation benefits from a "culture of work," is entitled to lifestyle choices, and enjoys life without undue intrusion by public agencies. Conversely, intergenerational transmission of poverty means little experience with the work culture, constrained lifestyle choices, and family intrusions endured in exchange for public benefits.

To reduce the future appearance of abuse we must reduce the current incidence of poverty. To ensure healthy child development, we must also assure that jobs for welfare recipients provide self-fulfillment and economic rewards.

Dr. Baumrind and policymakers agree that education, job training, and employment are antidotes to family violence. Economic stress, job loss, and income loss affect family functioning in critical ways: marital discord increases, and family members lose respect for unemployed adults.

Welfare reform should offer supports to public assistance recipients seeking to achieve gradual self-sufficiency, as well as to the working poor and the unemployed.

Child Abuse Prevention

Substantiated abuse requires evidence that parents have jeopardized the health and well-being of their children. More and more we have concerns about the escalating number of unsubstantiated protective services cases—families who have fallen below the standard of proof on multiple occasions. Of course, physical abuse is more easily substantiated *if* the existence of bodily injury or sexual contact is documented by medical examiners. At the other extreme is nonphysical abuse, where the body alone cannot tell the tale.

As policymakers have watched substantiations plateau and nonsubstantiations grow, they have begun to ask, "Why are high-risk families who repeatedly present themselves to the service system failing to receive *prevention* services?" The answers to this question create a rich policy agenda.

Prevention services have had discretionary rather than "hard money" funding mandates: Child welfare has a mandate to protect children by removals, mental health has a mandate to protect emotionally disturbed children by providing psychiatric care, and juvenile justice has a mandate to protect the public by rehabilitating offenders in residential settings. Few agencies have mandates to intervene early enough in families' lives to prevent the need for more extreme actions. There is, however, a growing consensus that early intervention, prevention, parenting, and family support programs are essential if abuse is to be reduced.

Optimal Parenting, Parenting Partnerships, and Parent Education

Dr. Baumrind's review assists us in appreciating the complexity of the question, What constitutes good or bad parenting?— especially as this unanswered question is juxtaposed with a kaleidoscope of opinions about children's rights to choose and to be protected.

Dr. Baumrind discusses the multiplicity of abuse-related parenting variables contained in the scholarly literature. Her summary allows us to imagine a near infinite number of permutations among the dimensions of responsiveness (warmth, reciprocity, attachment) and demandingness (coerciveness, confrontation, monitoring, supervision, consistent discipline, corporal punishment).

It is no wonder that public agencies entrusted with child protection responsibilities lack standards regarding when— beyond demonstrable physical abuse—legally actionable child maltreatment has occurred. Child protection in the 1990s is an art, with the judgment of abuse reflected in the eyes of various beholders such as judges, social workers, attorneys, children, the public, and parents themselves.

Moreover, prevention approaches such as "parent education" vary tremendously in emphasis, methodology, and outcome. This variance is attributable, in part, to the agency of origin, with public health programs focusing on nutrition and health; social services programs focusing on access to services and alternatives to corporal punishment; and mental health programs focusing on responses to DSM III diagnoses and related medications.

Parents, too, are unsure about how to raise their children in the 1990s. Cases presented to the public agencies more and more reflect a basic level of ignorance about how to parent effectively and the nature of parental obligations. Parents often know little about disciplinary strategies that are alternatives to physical punishment and/or verbal abuse.

Add to these uncertainties about parenting the fact that the number of working mothers with young children grew from 18% to 57% in the years between 1960 and 1987—and that there are federal proposals to mandate activity outside the home for most AFDC beneficiaries in the next decade (Lerner & Abrams, 1994).

Our growing reliance on paid caregivers means that questions of discipline and parenting now spill over into the laps of individuals who supervise children in their homes, in the child's home, in child care facilities, in schools, at camp, and, for latchkey or "home alone" children, by telephone.

These additive phenomena—lack of agreement on optimal parenting, no consensus on the content of parent education courses, virtual disappearance of intergenerational information on parenting, and a sharing of parenting with paid caregivers—point to a need for policy leadership.

Dr. Baumrind's research on parenting styles offers guidance to public policymakers who must respond to these shared-parenting realities. It confirms the need for public espousal of optimal principles of parenting, for parents and their paid surrogates to be educated equally about these parenting principles, and for social programs to be rooted in educated assumptions about how to expand the prevalence of positive parenting.

As regards the need for agreement on "what is good parenting," Dr. Baumrind offers the "authoritative" mode of parenting as effective with children across races and socio-economic levels. According to Dr. Baumrind, "The pattern of childrearing that has been shown by almost all investigators to be associated with optimal competence in middle-class white children, and also by some investigators with poor children of color . . . balance[s] what is asked of the child with what is offered to the child. This balanced style of child-rearing . . . requires a high investment of time and resources, reciprocity of rights and responsibilities in the parent-child relationship, a well-ordered regimen, and clarity of commu-nication" (p. 72).

In heeding this scholarly advice, policymakers should first see that parent education is expanded to include parent partnership education, that is, training of *all* caregivers involved with a child. Training for this expanded audience should focus on the behaviors associated with the authoritative approach and on techniques for applying the authoritative model in a way that is sensitive to a child's temperament, stage of development, and cultural background. Second, practitioners should note what to emphasize when assessing the strengths and weaknesses of families who have come to the attention of protective services.

Policymakers must acknowledge the truth of the African proverb that "it takes a village to raise a child." Integration of this ancient belief into our current understanding will allow decision makers to see that childrearing in the twenty-first century, of necessity, bonds parents and paid caregivers in a "parenting partnership."

Enhancing the Skills of Poor Parents

Dr. Baumrind's review shows us the variables most closely associated—in combination with poverty—with child abuse and neglect. This information can be translated into guidelines for agency staff who work with high-risk families. A few examples of how front line workers can be empowered by these scholarly findings are noted below.

Isolation

Research literature shows that abuse is reduced when poor parents enjoy access to support from a spouse or maternal grandmother. In addition, the literature underscores the importance of social supports associated with church attendance. Child protection staff should give adequate positive weight to these factors when assessing family functioning, and should offer social support resources to high-risk parents. Policymakers are advised to acknowledge and support kinship care, which allows close friends, as well as family members, to foster children. Too frequently kinship care fails to receive the same public support as substitute care.

Transience

Practitioners are also admonished to give special attention to the well-being of children in transient families who exploit other families, as these parents lack the secure emotional support and social competence that can serve as a buffer against child abuse (pp. 23–24).

Homelessness, in particular, is identified as a clearcut contributor to child abuse because of the stresses it presents to both adults and children. According to Baumrind, "Homeless children and their mothers generally endure hunger, insecurity, social isolation, elevated health problems (including infant mortality, low birth weight, immunization delays and infections), developmental delays, educational retardation, and behavioral and psychological problems" (p. 18).

Policymakers must move beyond their reliance on temporary housing as a response to homelessness. In order to counteract the deprivations and developmental lags associated with shelter life, public decision makers must invest in adequate low-income housing for chronically homeless parents with dependent children. In the meantime, the scholarly literature calls for shelters, improved educational/vocational linkages, physical security, health care, and social networking for shelter residents.

Threatening Neighborhoods

Research literature identifies the characteristics of neighborhoods—"hoods" where residents fear being exploited by one another—wherein poverty, social distrust, and lack of pride combine to heighten the probability of parental abuse (pp. 23–24).

Policymakers can learn from scholars that "low-risk" poor environments are possible if the following resources exist: "clean and decently maintained public housing, drug treatment programs . . . for all fertile women, low levels of noise and air pollution, and police officers who walk their community beat" (p. 19). Heeding this advice requires coordinated actions on the part of federal and state housing, substance abuse, environmental protection, and law enforcement officials.

Difficult Children

Research literature also points out that temperamentally challenging children, stepchildren, and adopted children frequently endure child abuse. Practitioners should take these factors into account when conducting investigations or assessing family functioning. Bedwetting, antisocial behavior, defiance, fights with siblings, or messing up are identified in the literature as indicators of potential parental maltreatment.

In this context, practitioners should be trained to compare their (neutral) perceptions of a child's behavior with those of parents who label the child—especially the adolescent—as "belligerent," "acting-out," or "defiant." Studies show that stressed parents often perceive child behavior more negatively than neutral observers, thus leading to "cycles of coercion" during which "parents lose their ability to control the child's behavior by other than threats and physical force" (p. 41).

Special preventive information, and appropriate referrals, should be offered to parents whose infants are irritable or hard to soothe, keeping in mind that low birth weight is a predictor of abuse only when parents are poor, isolated, and ill-informed.

Social workers are also advised to heed the potential for maltreatment and sexual abuse inherent in stepfather-stepdaughter relationships.

Finally, both policymakers and practitioners should remember that the characteristics of the environment, more than those of the individual, conduce to acts of violence against children. Once again, any attempt to prevent or extinguish child abuse must deal with the artifacts of poverty.

Conclusions

Policymakers must acknowledge their tendency to identify with *either* children *or* parents in designing and funding programs. Rarely do decision makers frame their goals and intentions so that the needs of both groups are addressed in a balanced manner.

By pointing out the documented interplay between parental circumstances and child development, Dr. Baumrind reinforces the message that interventions affect both parents and children regardless of how narrowly we might define the impact in the decision making process.

If we are to strengthen the fabric of child and family policy, researchers and decision makers must engage in an ongoing dialogue about what is known regarding current problems. Until now, this fabric has been gossamer-thin and dyed in black and white. By introducing the wealth of research results into our debates, we can weave a fabric whose richness, color, and texture will both reflect, and stand up to, the demands of the future.

References

Aber, J. L., Allen, J. P., Carlson, V., & Cicchetti, D. (1989). The effects of maltreatment on development during early childhood: Recent studies and their theoretical, clinical, and policy implications. In D. Cicchetti & V. Carlson (Eds.), *Child maltreatment: Theory and research on the causes and consequences of child abuse and neglect* (pp. 579–619). New York: Cambridge University Press.

Ahn, H. N., & Gilbert, N. (1992, September). Cultural diversity and sexual abuse prevention. *Social Service Review*, 410–427.

Ainsworth, M. D. S. (1977). Infant development and mother-infant interaction among the Ganda and American families. In P. H. Leiderman, S. R. Tulkin, & A. Rosenfeld (Eds.), *Culture and infancy* (pp. 119–149). New York: Academic.

Alexander, P. (1985). A systems conceptualization of incest. *Family Process, 24,* 79–88.

Alvy, K. T. (1987). *Black parenting.* New York: Irvington.

American Humane Society. (1983). *Highlights of official child neglect and abuse reporting.* Denver, CO: Author.

Aries, P. (1962). *Centuries of childhood.* New York: Vantage Books.

Azuma, H. (1986). Why study child development in Japan? In H. Sherman, H. Azuma, & K. Hakuta (Eds.), *Child development and education in Japan* (pp. 3–112). New York: W. H. Freeman.

Bandura, A. (1973). *Aggression: A social learning analysis.* New York: Prentice-Hall.

Barnett, W. S., & Escobar, C. M. (1990). Economic costs and benefits of early intervention. In S. J. Meisels & J. P. Shonkoff (Eds.), *Handbook of early childhood intervention* (pp. 560–582). New York: Cambridge University Press.

Baumrind, D. (1966). Effects of authoritative parental control on child behavior. *Child Development, 37*(4), 887–907.

Baumrind, D. (1967). Child care practices anteceding three patterns of preschool behavior. *Genetic Psychology Monographs, 75*, 43–88.

Baumrind, D. (1971a). Current patterns of parental authority. *Developmental Psychology Monographs, Part 2, 4*(1), 1–103.

Baumrind, D. (1971b). Harmonious parents and their preschool children. *Developmental Psychology, 4*(1), 99–102.

Baumrind, D. (1972). An exploratory study of socialization effects on black children: Some black-white comparisons. *Child Development, 43*(1), 261–267.

Baumrind, D. (1978a). Parental disciplinary patterns and social competence in children. *Youth and Society, 9*(3), 239–276.

Baumrind, D. (1978b). Reciprocal rights and responsibilities in parent-child relations. *Journal of Social Issues, 34*(2), 179–196.

Baumrind, D. (1983a). Rejoinder to Lewis's reinterpretation of parental firm control effects: Are authoritative parents really harmonious? *Psychological Bulletin, 94*(1), 132–142.

Baumrind, D. (1983b). Specious causal attributions in the social sciences: Heroin use as exemplar. *Journal of Personality and Social Psychology, 45*, 1289–1298.

Baumrind, D. (1989). Rearing competent children. In W. Damon (Ed.), *Child development today and tomorrow* (pp. 349–378). San Francisco: Jossey-Bass.

Baumrind, D. (1991a). Parenting styles and adolescent development. In R. Lerner, A. C. Petersen, & J. Brooks-Gunn (Eds.), *The encyclopedia on adolescence* (pp. 758–772). New York: Garland.

Baumrind, D. (1991b). The influence of parenting style on adolescent competence and substance abuse. *Journal of Early Adolescence, 11*(1), 56–94.

Baumrind, D. (1993). The average expectable environment is not good enough: A response to Scarr. *Child Development, 64*, 1299–1307.

Baumrind, D., & Black, A. E. (1967). Socialization practices associated with dimensions of competence in preschool boys and girls. *Child Development, 38*, 291–327.

Becker, W. C. (1964). Consequences of different kinds of parental discipline. In M. L. Hoffman & L. W. Hoffman (Eds.), *Review of child development research* (Vol. 1, pp. 169–208). New York: Russell Sage Foundation.

Bell, S. M., & Ainsworth, M. D. (1972). Infant crying and maternal responsiveness. *Child Development, 43*, 1171–1190.

Belle, D. (1982). Social ties and social support. In D. Belle (Ed.), *Lives in stress: Women and depression* (pp. 133–144). Beverly Hills, CA: Sage.

Belsky, J. (1980). Child maltreatment: An ecological integration. *American Psychologist, 35,* 320–335.

Belsky, J. (1991). Psychological maltreatment: Definitional limitations and unstated assumptions. *Development and Psychopathology, 3*(1), 31–36.

Belsky, J. (1993). Etiology of child maltreatment: A developmental-ecological analysis. *Psychological Bulletin, 114*(3), 413–434.

Belsky, J., Steinberg, L., & Draper, P. (1991). Childhood experience, interpersonal development, and reproductive strategy: An evolutionary theory of socialization. *Child Development, 62,* 647–670.

Belsky, J., & Vondra, J. (1989). Lessons from child abuse: The determinants of parenting. In D. Cicchetti & V. Carlson (Eds.), *Current research and theoretical advances in child maltreatment* (pp. 153–202). Cambridge: Cambridge University Press.

Belsky, J., Youngblade, L., & Pensky, E. (1990). Childrearing history, marital quality and maternal affect: Intergenerational transmission in a low-risk sample. *Development and Psychopathology, 1,* 294–304.

Berdie, J., & Wexler, S. (1984). Preliminary research on selected adolescent maltreatment issues: An analysis of supplemental data from the four adolescent maltreatment projects. *Adolescent maltreatment: Issues and program models,* National Center on Child Abuse and Neglect, Administration for Children, Youth, and Families, Office of Human Development Services, U.S. Department of Health and Human Services. Washington, DC: U.S. Government Printing Office.

Billings, A. G., & Moos, R. H. (1983). Comparisons of children of depressed and nondepressed parents: A social environmental perspective. *Journal of Abnormal Child Psychology, 11,* 463–486.

Blechman, E. (1982). Are children with one parent at psychological risk? A methodological review. *Journal of Marriage and the Family, 44,* 179–196.

Block, J. H., Block, J., & Gjerde, P. F. (1986). The personality of children prior to divorce: A prospective study. *Child Development, 57,* 827–840.

Block, J. H., Block, J., & Morrison, A. (1981). Parental agreement-disagreement on child-rearing orientations and gender-related personality correlates in children. *Child Development, 52,* 965–974.

Blumberg, M. L. (1974). Psychopathology of the abusing parent. *American Journal of Psychotherapy, 28,* 21–29.

Bowlby, J. (1969). *Attachment and loss:* Vol. 1, *Attachment.* New York: Basic Books.

Bowman, M., & Sigyardsson, S. (1990). Outcome in adoption: Lessons from longitudinal studies. In D. Brodzinsky & M. Schechter (Eds.), *The psychology of adoption* (pp. 93–106). New York: Oxford University Press.

Bronfenbrenner, U. (1985). Freedom and discipline across the decades. In G. Becker, H. Becker, & L. Huber (Eds.), *Ordnung und Unordnung* [Order and Disorder] (pp. 326–339). Weinheim, West Germany: Beltz Berlag.

Bugental, D. B., & Sherman, W. A. (1984). "Difficult" children as elicitors and targets of adult communication patterns: An attributional-behavioral transactional analysis. *Monographs of the Society for Research in Child Development, 49,* (Serial No. 205,1).

Burgess, R. L., & Conger, R. D. (1978). Family interaction in abusive, neglectful, and normal families. *Child Development, 49,* 1163–1173.

Burgess, R. L, & Draper, P. (1989). The explanation of family violence: The role of biological, behavioral, and cultural selection. In L. Ohlin & M. Tonry (Eds.), *Family violence. Crime and justice: A review of research, vol. 11* (pp. 59–116). Chicago, IL: University of Chicago Press.

Burton, R. V., & Whiting, J. W. M. (1961). The absent father and cross-sex identity. *Merrill-Palmer Quarterly of Behavior and Development, 7,* 85–95.

Cazenave, N., & Straus, M. (1979). Race, class, network embeddedness and family violence: A search for potent support systems. *Journal of Comparative Family Studies, 10,* 281–300.

Chasnoff, I., Landress, H., & Barrett, M. (1990). The prevalence of illicit drug or alcohol use during pregnancy and discrepancies in mandatory reporting in Pinellas County, Florida. *New England Journal of Medicine, 322,* 1202–1206.

Chilman, C. S. (1983). *Adolescent sexuality in a changing American society.* New York: John Wiley & Sons.

Child Abuse Prevention and Treatment Act. 42 U.S.C. §5101 (1974).

Children's Defense Fund (1991). *The state of America's children, 1991.* Washington, DC: Author.

Cicchetti, D. (1989). How research on child maltreatment has informed the study of child development: Perspectives from developmental psychopathology. In D. Cicchetti & V. Carlson (Eds.), *Child maltreatment: Theory and research on the causes and consequences of child abuse and neglect* (pp. 377–431). New York: Cambridge University Press.

Cicchetti, D. (1990). The organization and coherence of socioemotional, cognitive, and representational development: Illustrations through a developmental psychopathology perspective on Down syndrome and child maltreatment. In R. Thompson (Ed.), *Nebraska symposium on motivation:* Vol. 36, *Socioemotional development* (pp. 266–375). Lincoln: University of Nebraska Press.

Cicchetti, D., & Barnett, D. (1991). Toward the development of a scientific nosology of child maltreatment children. In D. Cicchetti & W. Grove (Eds.), *Thinking clearly about psychology: Essays in honor of Paul E. Meehl* (pp. 346–377). Minneapolis: University of Minnesota Press.

Cicchetti, D., Cummings, M., Greenberg, M., & Marvin, R. (1990). An organizational perspective on attachment beyond infancy: Implications for theory, measurement, and research. In M. Greenberg, D. Cicchetti, & M. Cummings (Eds.), *Attachment in the preschool years: Theory, research and intervention* (pp. 3–49). Chicago: University of Chicago Press.

Cicchetti, D., & Rizley, F. (1981). Developmental perspectives on the etiology, intergenerational transmission, and sequelae of child maltreatment. *New directions for child development,* Vol.11, *Developmental perspective on child maltreatment* (pp. 31–55). San Francisco: Jossey-Bass.

Cicchetti, D., & Sroufe, L. A. (1978). An organizational view of affect: Illustration from the study of Down's syndrome infants. In M. Lewis & L. Rosenblum (Eds.), *The development of affect* (pp. 309–350). New York: Plenum.

Clark, R. (1983). *Family life and school achievement: Why poor black children succeed or fail.* Chicago: University of Chicago Press.

Cochran, M., & Brassard, J. (1979). Child development and personal social networks. *Child Development, 50,* 601–616.

Cochrane, W. A. (1965). The battered child syndrome. *Canadian Journal of Public Health, 56,* 193–196.

Colletta, N. (1981). Social support and the risk of maternal rejection by adolescent mothers. *Journal of Psychology, 109,* 191–197.

Conger, R. D., Conger, K. J., Elder, G. H., Jr., Lorenz, F. O., Simons, R. L., & Whitbeck, L. B. (1992). A family process model of economic hardship and adjustment of early adolescent boys. *Child Development, 63,* 526–541.

Conger, R. D., McCarty, J., Yang, R., Lahey, B., & Kropp, J. (1984). Perception of child, childrearing values, and emotional distress as mediating links between environmental stressors and observed maternal behavior. *Child Development, 54,* 2234–2247.

Cowan, C. P., & Cowan, P. A. (1992). *When partners become parents.* New York: Basic Books.

Creighton, S. (1985). Epidemiological study of abused children and their families in the United Kingdom between 1977 and 1982. *Child Abuse and Neglect, 9,* 441–448.

Crittenden, P. (1985a). Social networks, quality of childrearing, and child development. *Child Development, 56,* 1299–1313.

Crittenden, P. (1985b). Maltreated infants: Vulnerability and resilience. *Journal of Child Psychology and Psychiatry, 26,* 85–96.

Crittenden, P. (1988). Relationships at risk. In J. Belsky & T. Nezworski (Eds.), *Clinical implications of attachment* (pp. 136–174). Hillsdale, NJ: Erlbaum.

Crnic, K. A., Greenberg, M. T., Ragozin, N. M., Robinson, N. M., & Basham, R. B. (1983). Effects of stress and social support on mothers of premature and full-term infants. *Child Development, 54,* 209–217.

Crnic, K., & Greenberg, M. (1987). Maternal stress, social support, and coping: Influences on the early mother-child relationship. In C. Boukydis (Ed.), *Research on support for parents and infants in the postnatal period* (pp. 25–40). Norwood, NJ: Ablex.

Crockenberg, S. (1987). Support for adolescent mothers during the postnatal period: Theory and research. In C. Boukydis (Ed.), *Research on support for parents and infants in the post-natal period* (pp. 3–24). Norwood, NJ: Ablex.

Cummings, E. M., Ballard, M., & El-Sheikh, M. (1991). Responses of children and adolescents to interadult anger as a function of gender, age, and mode of expression. *Merrill-Palmer Quarterly, 37,* 543–560.

Cummings, E. M., Iannotti, R. J., & Zahn-Waxler, C. (1985). The influence of conflict between adults on the emotions and aggression of young children. *Developmental Psychology, 21,* 495–507.

Cummings, E. M., & Zahn-Waxler, C. (1992). Emotions and the socialization of aggression: Adults' angry behavior and children's arousal and aggression. In A. Fraczek & H. Zumkley (Eds.), *Socialization and aggression* (pp. 61–84). New York and Heidelberg: Springer-Verlag.

Dail, P. W. (1990). The psychosocial context of homeless mothers with young children: Program and policy implications. *Child Welfare, 64,* 291–307.

deMause, L. (Ed.) (1974). *The history of childhood.* New York: The Psychohistory Press.

Dornbusch, S. M., Ritter, P. L., Leiderman, P. H., Roberts, D. J., & Fraleigh, M. J. (1987). The relation of parenting style to adolescent performance. *Child Development, 58,* 1244–1257.

Drillien, C. M. (1964). *The growth and development of the prematurely born infant.* Baltimore: Williams & Wilkins.

Dunn, J. (1988). *The beginnings of social understanding.* Cambridge, MA: Harvard University Press.

Easson, W. (1973, July). Special sexual problems of the adopted adolescent. *Medical Aspects of Human Sexuality, 7*(7), 92–105.

Edelman, M. W. (1987). *Families in peril: An agenda for social change.* Cambridge, MA: Harvard University Press.

Egeland, B. (1988). Breaking the cycle of abuse: Implications for prediction and intervention. In K. D. Browne, C. Davies, & P. Stratton (Eds.), *Early prediction and prevention of child abuse* (pp. 87–99). New York: John Wiley & Sons.

Egeland, B., & Erickson, M. F. (1987). Psychologically unavailable caregiving: The effects on development of young children and the implications for intervention. In M. Brassard, S. Hart, & B. Germain (Eds.), *Psychological maltreatment of children and youth* (pp. 110–120). New York: Pergamon Press.

Egeland, B., Jacobvitz, D., & Sroufe, L. A. (1988). Breaking the cycle of abuse: Relationship predictors. *Child Development, 59*(42), 1080–1088.

Egeland, B., & Sroufe, L. A. (1981a). Attachment and early maltreatment. *Child Development, 52,* 44–52.

Egeland, B., & Sroufe, L. A. (1981b). Developmental sequelae of maltreatment in infancy. *New directions for child development:*

Vol. 11, *Developmental perspective on child maltreatment,* (pp. 77–92). San Francisco: Jossey-Bass.

Egeland, B., Sroufe, L. A., & Erickson, M. (1983). The developmental consequences of different patterns of maltreatment. *Journal of Child Abuse and Neglect, 7,* 459–469.

Eisenberg, N. (1992). *The caring child.* Cambridge, MA: Harvard University Press.

Elder, G. H., Jr. (1974). *Children of the Great Depression.* Chicago: University of Chicago Press.

Elder, G. H., Jr., Caspi, A., & Nguyen, T. V. (1986). Resourceful and vulnerable children: Family influence in hard times. In R. K. Silbereisen, K. Eyferth, & G. Rudinger (Eds.), *Development as action in context* (pp. 167–186). New York: Springer-Verlag.

Elder, G. H., Jr., Nguyen, T. V., & Caspi, A. (1985). Linking family hardship to children's lives. *Child Development, 56,* 361–375.

Ellis, R. H., & Milner, J. S. (1981). Child abuse and locus of control. *Psychological Reports, 48,* 507–510.

Elmer, E. (1967). *Children in jeopardy: A case of abused minors and their families.* Pittsburgh, PA: University of Pittsburgh Press.

Elmer, E. (1977). A follow-up study of traumatized children. *Pediatrics, 59,* 273.

Emery, R. E. (1982). Interparental conflict and the children of discord and divorce. *Psychological Bulletin, 92,* 310–330.

Erickson, M. F., Egeland, B., & Pianta, R. (1989). The effects of maltreatment on the development of young children. In D. Cicchetti & V. Carlson (Eds.), *Theory and research on the causes and consequences of child abuse and neglect* (pp. 647–684). New York: Cambridge University Press.

Eron, L. (1982). Parent-child interaction, television violence, and aggression of children. *American Psychologist, 37*(2), 197–211.

Farber, E. A., & Egeland, B. (1987). Invulnerability among abused and neglected children. In E. J. Anthony & B. Cohler (Eds.), *The invulnerable child* (pp. 253–288). New York: Guilford Press.

Farson, R. (1974). *Birthrights.* New York: Macmillan.

Field, T., Widmayer, S., Stringer, S., & Ignatoff, E. (1980). Teenage, lower-class black mothers and their preterm infants: An intervention and developmental followup. *Child Development, 51,* 426–436.

Final report of youth and America's future. (1988, November). The William T. Grant Foundation Commission on Work, Family and Citizenship.

Finkelhor, D. (1984). *Child sexual abuse: New theory and research.* New York: Free Press.

Finkelhor, D., & Lewis, I. A. (1988). An epidemiologic approach to the study of child molestation. In R. A. Prentky & V. L. Quinsey (Eds.), *Human sexual aggression: Current perspectives* (pp. 64–78). New York: New York Academy of Sciences.

Fontana, V. J. (1968). Further reflections on maltreatment of children. *New York Journal of Medicine, 68,* 2214–2215.

Fraiberg, S., Edelson, E., & Shapiro, V. (1980). Ghosts in the nursery: A psychoanalytical approach to the problems of impaired infant-mother relationships. In S. Fraiberg & L. Fraiberg (Eds.), *Clinical studies in infant mental health the first year of life* (pp. 164–196). New York: Basic Books.

Franklin, B. (1986). *The rights of children.* Oxford: Basil Blackwell.

Friedman, S. (1988). A family systems approach to treatment. In L. E. A. Walker (Ed.), *Handbook on sexual abuse of children: Assessment and treatment issues* (pp. 326–349). New York: Springer.

Friedrich, W. N., & Wheeler, K. K. (1982). The abusing parent revisited: A decade of psychological research. *Journal of Nervous and Mental Disease, 10,* 577–587.

Fuchs, V. R., & Reklis, D. M. (1992). America's children: Economic perspectives and policy options. *Science, 255,* 41–46.

Furstenberg, F. F. (1976). *Unplanned parenthood: The social consequences of teenage childbearing.* New York: Macmillan.

Furstenberg, F., Brooks-Gunn, J., & Morgan, S. (1987). *Adolescent mothers in later life.* New York: Cambridge University Press.

Furstenberg, F., Lincoln, R., & Menken, J. (Eds.) (1981). *Teenage sexuality, pregnancy, and childbearing.* Philadelphia: University of Pennsylvania Press.

Garbarino, J. (1976). A preliminary study of some ecological correlates of child abuse: The impact of socioeconomic stress on mothers. *Child Development, 47,* 178–198.

Garbarino, J. (1990, January). Draft: *Adolescent victims of maltreatment.* Prepared for U.S. Congress, Office of Technology Assessment.

Garbarino, J., & Sherman, D. (1980). High-risk neighborhoods and high-risk families: The human ecology of child maltreatment. *Child Development, 51,* 188–198.

Gecas, V. (1979). The influence of social class on socialization. In W. Burr, R. Hill, F. Nye, & I. Reiss (Eds.), *Contemporary theories about the family: Research-based theories* (Vol. 1, pp. 365–404). New York: Free Press.

Gelles, R. J. (1974). *The violent home: A study of physical aggression between husbands and wives.* Beverly Hills, CA: Sage.

Gelles, R. J. (1989). Child abuse and violence in single-parent families: Parent absence and economic deprivation. *American Journal of Orthopsychiatry, 59,* 492–501.

Gelles, R. J., & Edfeldt, A. W. (1986). Violence towards children in the United States and Sweden. *Child Abuse and Neglect, 10,* 501–510.

Gelles, R. J., & Harrop, J. W. (1991). The risk of abusive violence among children with nongenetic caretakers. *Family Relations, 40,* 78–83.

Gelles, R. J., & Straus, M. A. (1988). *Intimate violence.* New York: Simon & Schuster.

Gil, D. (1970). *Violence against children.* Cambridge, MA: Harvard University Press.

Gil, D. (1975). Unraveling child abuse. *American Journal of Orthopsychiatry, 45,* 346–356.

Gilbert, N., Berrick, J. D., Leprohn, N., & Nyman, N. (1989). *Protecting young children from sexual abuse.* Lexington, MA: Lexington Books.

Giovannoni, J. (1991). Social policy considerations in defining psychological maltreatment. *Development and Psychopathology, 3*(1), 51–59.

Giovannoni, J., & Billingsley, A. (1970). Child neglect among the poor: A study of parental adequacy in families of three ethnic groups. *Child Welfare, 49,* 196.

Glazer, N., & Moynihan, D. P. (1965). *Beyond the melting pot.* Cambridge, MA: MIT Press.

Goldstein, J., Freud, A., & Solnit, A. (1979). *Before the best interests of the child.* New York: Free Press.

Goldstein, M. J., & Rodnick, E. H. (1975). The family's contribution to schizophrenia: Current status. *Schizophrenia Bulletin, 1,* 48–63.

Goodman, P. (1964). *Compulsory mis-education.* New York: Horizon.

Gould, S. J. (1980). Sociobiology and the theory of natural selection. In G. W. Barlow & J. Silverberg (Eds.), *Sociobiology: Beyond nature/nurture* (pp. 257–269). Boulder, CO: Westview Press.

Grusec, J. E. (1983). The internalization of altruistic dispositions: A cognitive analysis. In E. T. Higgins, D. N. Ruble, & W. W. Hartup (Eds.), *Social cognition and social development* (pp. 275–293). New York: Cambridge University Press.

Grusec, J. E., & Lytton, H. (1988). *Social development: History, theory, and research.* New York: Springer-Verlag.

Grych, J. H., & Fincham, F. D. (1990). Marital conflict and children's adjustment: A cognitive-contextual framework. *Psychological Bulletin, 108,* 267–290.

Haley, J. (1976). *Problem-solving therapy.* San Francisco: Jossey-Bass.

Hamburg, B. A., & Dixon, S. L. (1992). Adolescent Pregnancy and Parenthood. In M. K. Rosenheim & M. F. Testa (Eds.), *Early Parenthood and Coming of Age in the 1900s* (pp. 17–33). New Brunswick, NJ: Rutgers University Press.

Hampton, R. L., & Newberger, E. H. (1985). Child abuse incidence and reporting by hospitals: Significance of severity, class, and race. *American Journal of Public Health, 75,* 56–60.

Hauswald, L. (1987). External pressure/internal change: Child neglect on the Navajo reservation. In N. Scheper-Hughes (Ed.), *Child survival: Anthropological perspectives on the treatment and maltreatment of children* (pp. 145–164). Boston: D. Reidel.

Healthy children: Investing in the future. (1988, February). U.S. Congress, Office of Technology Assessment, OTA-H-345. Washington, DC: U.S. Government Printing Office.

Herrenkohl, R. C., & Herrenkohl, E. C. (1981). Some antecedents and developmental consequences of child maltreatment. In R. Rizley & D. Cicchetti (Eds.), *New directions for child development: Vol. II, Developmental perspectives on child maltreatment* (pp. 57–76). San Francisco: Jossey-Bass.

Herrenkohl, R. C., Herrenkohl, E. C., & Egolf, B. P. (1983). Circumstances surrounding the occurrence of child maltreatment. *Journal of Consulting and Clinical Psychology, 51*(3), 424–431.

Hess, R. D., & Camara, K. A. (1979). Post-divorce family relationships as mediating factors in the consequences of divorce for children. *Journal of Social Issues, 35,* 79–96.

Hetherington, E. M. (1972). Effects of father absence on personality development in adolescent daughters. *Developmental Psychology, 7*, 313–326.

Hetherington, E. M., Cox, M. J., & Cox, R. (1982). Effects of divorce on parents and children. In M. E. Lamb (Ed.), *Nontraditional families* (pp. 233–288). Hillsdale, NJ: Erlbaum.

Hetherington, E. M., Cox, M. J., & Cox, R. (1985). Long-term effects of divorce and remarriage on the adjustment of children. *Journal of the American Academy of Psychiatry, 24*(5), 518–530.

Hetherington, E. M., & Clingempeel, W. G. (in collaboration with Anderson, E. R., Deal, J. E., Hagan, M. S., Hollier, E. A., & Lindner, M. S.). (1992). Coping with marital transitions. *Monographs of the Society for Research in Child Development, 57* (Nos. 2–3).

Hetherington, E. M., Stanley-Hagan, M., & Anderson, E. (1989). Marital transitions: A child's perspective. *American Psychologist, 44*, 303–312.

Hill, R. B. (1972). *The strengths of black families.* New York: Emerson Hall.

Hinde, R. A. (1974). *Biological bases of social behavior.* New York: McGraw-Hill.

Hoffman, M. L. (1963). Parent discipline and the child's consideration for others. *Child Development, 34*, 573–588.

Hoffman, M. L. (1970a). Conscience, personality and socialization techniques. *Human Development, 13*, 90–126.

Hoffman, M. L. (1970b). Moral development. In P. H. Mussen (Ed.), *Carmichael's manual of child psychology* (3rd ed., Vol. 2, pp. 261–360). New York: John Wiley & Sons.

Hoffman, M. L. (1983). Affective and cognitive processes in moral internalization. In E. G. Higgins, D. N. Ruble, & W. W. Hartup (Eds.), *Social cognition and social development* (pp. 236–254). New York: Cambridge University Press.

Hoffman, M. L., Rosen, S., & Lippitt, R. (1960). Parental coerciveness, child autonomy, and child's role at school. *Sociometry, 23*, 15–22.

Hogan, P. T., & Siu, S. F. (1988). Minority children and the child welfare system: An historical perspective. *Social Work, 33*(6), 493–498.

Holt, J. (1974). *Escape from childhood: The needs and rights of children.* New York: E. P. Dutton.

Homans, G. C. (1967). Fundamental social processes. In N. J. Smelser (Ed.), *Sociology: An introduction* (pp. 29–78). New York: John Wiley & Sons.

Israel, A. C., & Brown, M. S. (1979). Effects of directiveness of instructions and surveillance on the production and persistence of children's donations. *Journal of Experimental Child Psychology, 27*, 250–261.

Jackson, J. F. (1993a). Human behavioral genetics, Scarr's theory, and her views on interventions: A critical review and commentary on their implications for African American children. *Human Development, 64*, 1318–1332.

Jackson, J. F. (1993b). Multiple caregiving among African Americans and infant attachment: The need for an emic approach. *Human Development, 36*, 87–102.

Johannesson, I. (1974). Aggressive behavior among school children related to maternal practices in early childhood. In J. de Wit & W. W. Hartup (Eds.), *Determinants and origins of aggressive behavior* (pp. 413–425). The Hague: Mouton.

Johnston, J. (1990). Role diffusion and role reversal: Structural variations in divorced families and children's functioning. *Family Relations, 39*, 405–413.

Justice, B., & Justice, R. (1979). *The broken taboo: Sex in the family.* New York: Human Sciences Press.

Kadushin, A., & Martin, J. (1981). *Child abuse—An interactional event.* New York: Columbia University Press.

Kagan, J., & Moss, H. A. (1962). *Birth to maturity: A study in psychological development.* New York: John Wiley & Sons.

Kaufman, J., & Zigler, E. (1987). Do abused children become abusive parents? *American Journal of Orthopsychiatry, 57*(2), 186–192.

Kellam, S., Ensminger, M. E., & Turner, R. (1977). Family structure and the mental health of children. *Archives of General Psychiatry, 34*, 1012–1022.

Kempe, C. H. (1973). A practical approach to the protection of the abused child and rehabilitation of the abusing parent. *Pediatrics, 51*(Pt. 3), 804–812.

Kempe, C. H., Silverman, F. N., Steele, B. F., Droegemueller, W., & Silver, H. R. (1962). The battered child syndrome. *Journal of the American Medical Association, 181*, 17–24.

Kinard, E. M., & Klerman, L. F. (1980). Teenage parenting and child abuse: Are they related? *American Journal of Orthopsychiatry, 50*(3), 481–488.

Klein, M., & Stern, L. (1971). Low birth weight and the battered child syndrome. *American Journal of Diseases of Children, 122,* 15–18.

Kohn, M. (1977). *Class and conformity* (2nd ed.). Chicago: University of Chicago Press.

Korbin, J. (1987). Child sexual abuse: Implication from the cross-cultural record. In N. Scheper-Hughes (Ed.), *Child survival: Anthropological perspectives on the treatment and maltreatment of children* (pp. 247–265). Boston: D. Reidel.

Lally, R. J., Mangione, P. L., & Honig, A. S. (1988). The Syracuse University Family Development Research Program: Long-range impact on an early intervention with low-income children and their families. In D. Powell (Ed.), *Parent education as early childhood intervention: Emerging directions in theory, research and practice* (pp. 79–104). Norwood, NJ: Ablex.

Lamb, M., & Easterbrooks, M. A. (1981). Individual differences in parental sensitivity: Origins, components, and consequences. In M. Lamb & L. Sherrod (Eds.), *Infant social cognition: Empirical and theoretical considerations* (pp. 127–153). Hillsdale, NJ: Erlbaum.

Lazar, I., Hubbell, V., Murray, H., Rosche, M., & Royce, J. (1977, September). *The persistence of preschool effects: A long-term follow-up of fourteen infant and preschool experiments.* (Final Report for ACYR Grant No. 18–76–0783). Ithaca, NY: Cornell University, Community Service Laboratory.

Lefkowitz, M., Eron, L., Walder, L., & Huesmann, L. (1977). *Growing up to be violent: A longitudinal study of the development of aggression.* New York: Pergamon.

Lempers, J., Clark-Lempers, D., & Simons, R. (1989). Economic hardship, parenting, and distress in adolescence. *Child Development, 60,* 25–49.

Lepper, M. (1981). Intrinsic and extrinsic motivation in children: Detrimental effects of superfluous social controls. In W. A. Collins (Ed.), *Aspects of the development of competence: The Minnesota symposium on child psychology* (Vol. 14, pp. 155–214). Hillsdale, NJ: Erlbaum.

Lepper, M. (1983). Social control processes and the internalization of social values: An attributional perspective. In E. T. Higgins, D. N. Ruble, & W. W. Hartup (Eds.), *Social cognition and social development* (pp. 294–330). New York: Cambridge University Press.

Lerner, R. M. (1991). Changing organism—context relations as the basic process of development: A developmental-contextual perspective. *Developmental Psychology, 27,* 27–32.

Lerner, R. (1992). *Final solutions.* University Park, PA: Pennsylvania State University Press.

Lerner, J. V., & Abrams, L. A. (1994). Developmental correlates of maternal employment influences on children. In C. B. Fisher & R. M. Lerner (Eds.), *Applied developmental psychology* (pp. 174–206). New York: McGraw-Hill.

LeVine, R. A., & LeVine, S. E. (1966). *Nyansongo: A Gusti community in Kenya.* New York: John Wiley & Sons.

Lewontin, R. (1991). *Biology as ideology: The doctrine of DNA.* Concord, Ontario, Canada; Anansi Press.

Libby, P., & Bybee, R. (1979). The physical abuse of adolescents. *Journal of Social Issues, 35,* 101–126.

Loftus, E. (1993). The reality of repressed memories. *American Psychologist, 48,* 518–537.

Lucier, J. P. (1992). Unconventional rights: Children and the United Nations. *Family Policy, 5*(3). Washington, DC: Family Research Council.

Lynch, M., & Roberts, J. (1977). Predicting child abuse: Signs of bonding failure in the maternity hospital. *British Medical Journal, 1*(6061), 624–626.

Maccoby, E. E., & Martin, J. A. (1983). Socialization in the context of the family: Parent-child interaction. In E. M. Hetherington (Ed.), P. H. Mussen (Series Ed.), *Handbook of child psychology: Vol. 4. Socialization, personality, and social development* (pp. 1–101). New York: John Wiley & Sons.

MacDonald, K. (1992). Warmth as a developmental construct: An evolutionary analysis. *Child Development, 63*(4), 753–773.

Main, M., & Goldwyn, R. (1984). Predicting rejection of her infant from mother's representation of her own experience: Implications for the abused-abusing intergenerational cycle. *Child Abuse and Neglect, 8,* 203–217.

Main, M., & Solomon, J. (1986). Discovery of a disorganized disoriented attachment pattern. In T. B. Brazelton & M. W. Yogman (Eds.), *Effective development in infancy* (pp. 95–124). Norwood, NJ: Ablex.

Martin, E. P., & Martin, J. M. (1978). *The black extended family*. Chicago: University of Chicago Press.

Martin, J. A. (1981). A longitudinal study of the consequences of early mother-infant interaction: A microanalytic approach. *Monographs of the Society for Research in Child Development, 46*(3, Serial No. 190).

Masten, A. S. (1992). Homeless children in the United States: Mark of a nation at risk. *Current Directions in Psychological Science, 1*(2), 41–44.

Masten, A. S., & Garmezy, N. (1985). Risk, vulnerability, and protective factors in developmental psychopathology. In B. B. Lahey & A. E. Kazdin (Eds.), *Advances in clinical child psychology* Vol. 8, (pp. 1–52). New York: Plenum.

McCord, J. (1979). Some child-rearing antecedents of criminal behavior in adult men. *Journal of Personality and Social Psychology, 37*(9), 1477–1486.

McDonald, A. D. (1964). Intelligence in children of very low birth weight. *British Journal of Preventive and Social Medicine, 18*, 59–74.

McGee, R. A., & Wolfe, D. A. (1991). Psychological maltreatment: Toward an operational definition. *Development and Psychopathology, 3*(1), 3–18.

McLanahan, S. S. (1994). The consequences of single motherhood. *The American Prospect, 18*, 48–58.

McLoyd, V. C. (1990). The impact of economic hardship on black families and children: Psychological distress, parenting, and socioemotional development. *Child Development, 61*, 311–346.

McLoyd, V. C., & Wilson, L. (1990). Maternal behavior, social support, and economic conditions as predictors of distress in children. In V. C. McLoyd & C. A. Flanagan (Eds.), *Economic stress: Effects on family life and child development* (pp. 49–69). San Francisco: Jossey-Bass.

Melnick, B., & Hurley, J. (1969). Distinctive personality attributes of child-abusing mothers. *Journal of Consulting and Clinical Psychology, 33*, 746–749.

Milburn, N., & D'Ercole, A. (1991). Homeless women: Moving toward a comprehensive model. *American Psychologist, 46*, 1161–1169.

Millar, W. S. (1972). A study of operant conditioning under delayed reinforcement in early infancy. *Monographs of the Society for Research in Child Development, 37*(2).

Miller, D. S. (1959). Fractures among children. *Minnesota Medicine, 42,* 1209–1213.

Milner, J. S. (1988). An ego-strength scale for the Child Abuse Potential Inventory. *Journal of Family Violence, 3,* 151–162.

Minuchin, P. (1985). Families and individual development: Provocations from the field of family therapy. *Child Development, 56,* 289–302.

Minuchin, S. (1974). *Families and family therapy.* Cambridge, MA: Harvard University Press.

Molnar, M. J., Rath, W. R., & Klein, T. P. (1990). Constantly compromised: The impact of homelessness on children. *Journal of Social Issues, 46*(4), 109–124.

Morse, C., Sahler, O., & Friedman, S. (1970). A three-year follow-up study of abused and neglected children. *American Journal of Diseases of Children, 120,* 439–446.

Murphy, S., Orkow, B., & Nicola, R. (1985). Predictions of child abuse and neglect: A prospective study. *Child Abuse and Neglect, 9,* 225–235.

National Center on Child Abuse and Neglect. (1988). *Study findings: Study of National Incidence and Prevalence of Child Abuse and Neglect: 1988.* Washington, DC: U.S. Department of Health and Human Services, Office of Human Development Services, Administration for Children, Youth, and Families, Children's Bureau.

National Urban League. (about 1973). *When the marching stopped: An analysis of black issues in the '70s.* New York: National Urban League.

Neill, A. S. (1964). *Summerhill.* New York: Hart.

Newberger, C. M. (1980). The cognitive structure of parenthood: Designing a descriptive measure. *New Directions for Child Development, 7,* 45–67.

Newberger, C. M., Melnicoe, L. H., & Newberger, E. H. (1986). The American family in crisis: Implications for children. *Current Problems in Pediatrics, 16* (Whole No. 12).

Ogbu, J. (1981). Origins of human competence: A cultural-ecological perspective. *Child Development, 52,* 413–429.

Olds, D. L. (1988). The prenatal/early infancy project. In E. L. Cowen, R. P. Lorion, & J. Ramos-McKay (Eds.), *Fourteen ounces of prevention: A handbook for practitioners* (pp. 9–22). Washington, DC: American Psychological Association.

Olweus, D. (1980). Familial and temperamental determinants of aggressive behavior in adolescent boys: A causal analysis. *Developmental Psychology, 16,* 644–666.

Orraschel, H., Weissman, M. M., & Kidd, K. K. (1980). Children and depression: The children of depressed parents; the childhood of depressed parents; depression in children. *Journal of Affective Disorders, 2*(1), 1–16.

Parke, R. D., & Collmer, C. (1975). Child abuse: An interdisciplinary analysis. In E. M. Hetherington (Ed.), *Review of child development research* (Vol. 5, pp. 509–590). Chicago: University of Chicago Press.

Parke, R. D., & Slaby, R. G. (1983). The development of aggression. In E. M. Hetherington (Ed.), P. H. Mussen (Series Ed.), *Handbook of child psychology: Vol. 4. Socialization, personality, and social development* (pp. 547–641). New York: John Wiley & Sons.

Parker, G., Tupling, H., & Brown, L. B. (1979). A parental bonding instrument. *British Journal of Medical Psychology, 52,* 1–10.

Parpal, M., & Maccoby, E. E. (1985). Maternal responsiveness and subsequent child compliance. *Child Development, 56,* 1326–1334.

Patterson, G. (1980). Mothers: The unacknowledged victims. *Monograph of the Society for Research in Child Development,* Serial No. 186.

Patterson, G. (1982). *Coercive family process:* Vol. 3, *A social learning approach.* Eugene, OR: Castalia.

Patterson, G. (1986). Performance models for antisocial boys. *American Psychologist, 41,* 432–444.

Patterson, G., & Capaldi, D. M. (1991). Antisocial parents: Unskilled and vulnerable. In P. Cowan & E. M. Hetherington (Eds.), *The effect of transitions on families* (pp. 195–218). Hillsdale, NJ: Erlbaum.

Pearce, D. (1990). Welfare is not for women: Why the war on poverty cannot conquer the feminization of poverty. In L. Gordon (Ed.), *Women, the state, and welfare* (pp. 265–279). Madison, WI: University of Wisconsin Press.

Pelton, L. H. (Ed.). (1985). *The social context of child abuse and neglect.* New York: Human Sciences Press.

Peters, M. F. (1976). *Nine black families: A study of household management and childrearing in black families with working mothers.* Ann Arbor, MI: University Microfilms.

Peters, M., & Massey, G. (1983). Mundane extreme environmental stress in family stress theories: The case of black families in white America. *Marriage and Family Review, 6,* 193–218.

Phares, E. J. (1976). *Locus of control in personality.* Morristown, NJ: General Learning Press.

Polansky, N. A., Borgman, R. D., & DeSaix, C. (1972). *Roots of futility.* San Francisco: Jossey-Bass.

Polansky, N. A., Chalmers, M. A., Buttenwieser, E., & Williams, D. P. (1981). *Damaged parents.* Chicago: University of Chicago Press.

Purdy, L. M. (1992). *In their best interest?* Ithaca, NY: Cornell University Press.

Radke-Yarrow, M., Cummings, E. M., Kuczynski, L., & Chapman, M. (1985). Patterns of attachment in two- and three-year-olds in normal families and families with parental depression. *Child Development, 56,* 884–893.

Reid, J. B., Kavanaugh, K., & Baldwin, D. V. (1987). Abusive parents' perceptions of child problem behaviors: An example of parental bias. *Journal of Abnormal Child Psychology, 15,* 457–466.

Rivara, F. P., Kamitsuka, M. D., & Quan, L. (1988). Injuries to children younger than 1 year of age. *Pediatrics, 81,* 93–97.

Robertson, M. J. (1991). Homeless women with children. *American Psychologist, 46*(11), 1198–1204.

Robson, K. S., & Moss, H. A. (1970). Patterns and determinants of maternal attachment. *Journal of Pediatrics, 77,* 976–985.

Rogers, C. R. (1960). A therapist's view of personal goals. *Pendle Hill Pamphlet 108.* Wallingford, PA: Pendle Hill.

Rohner, R. P. (1975). *They love me, they love me not.* New Haven, CT: Human Relations Area Files.

Rollins, B. C., & Thomas, D. L. (1975). A theory of parental power and child compliance. In R. E. Cromwell & D. H. Oldson (Eds.), *Power in families* (pp. 38–60). Beverly Hills, CA: Sage.

Rosen, B. C., & D'Andrade, R. (1959). The psychological origins of achievement motivation. *Sociometry, 22,* 185–218.

Rutter, M. (1979). Protective factors in children's responses to stress and disadvantage. In M. Kent & J. Rolf (Eds.), *Primary prevention of psychopathology* (Vol. 3, pp. 49–74). Hanover, NH: University Press of New England.

Rutter, M. (1987). Psychosocial resilience and protective mechanisms. *American Journal of Orthopsychiatry, 57,* 316–331.

Sameroff, A. J., Barocas, R., & Seifer, R. (1984). The early development of children born to mentally-ill women. In N. F. Watt, E. J. Anthony, L. C. Wynn, & J. Rolf (Eds.), *Children at risk for schizophrenia: A longitudinal perspective* (pp. 482–514). New York: Cambridge University Press.

Sameroff, A. J., & Chandler, M. J. (1975). Reproductive risk and the continuum of caretaking casualty. In F. D. Horowitz, M. Hetherington, S. Scarr-Salapatek, & G. Siegel (Eds.), *Review of child development research* (Vol. 4, pp. 187–244). Chicago: University of Chicago Press.

Sameroff, A. J., & Fiese, B. H. (1990). Transactional regulation and early intervention. In S. J. Meisels & J. P. Shonkoff (Eds.), *Handbook of early childhood intervention* (pp. 119–149). New York: Cambridge University Press.

Scarr, S. (1992). Developmental theories for the 1990s: Development and individual differences. *Child Development, 63,* 1–19.

Scheper-Hughes, N. (Ed.) (1987). *Child survival: Anthropological perspectives on the treatment and maltreatment of children.* Boston: D. Reidel.

Schaefer, E. S. (1959). A circumplex model for maternal behavior. *Journal of Abnormal and Social Psychology, 59,* 226–235.

Schuck, J. R. (1974). The use of causal nonexperimental models in aggression research. In J. de Wit & W. W. Hartup (Eds.), *Determinants and origins of aggressive behavior* (pp. 381–389). The Hague: Mouton.

Schutzman, D., Frankenfield-Chernicoff, M., Clatterbaugh, H., & Singer, J. (1991). Incidence of intrauterine cocaine exposure in a suburban setting. *Pediatrics, 88,* 825–827.

Sears, R. (1961). Relation of early socialization experiences to aggression in middle childhood. *Journal of Abnormal and Social Psychology, 63*(3), 466–492.

Seitz, V., Rosenbaum, L. K., & Apfel, N. H. (1985). Effects of family support intervention: A 10-year follow-up. *Child Development, 56,* 376–391.

Select Committee on Children, Youth, and Families, U.S. House of Representatives, One Hundred First Congress, First Session. (1989, November). No place to call home: Discarded children in America. Washington, DC: U.S. Government Printing Office.

Simons, R. L., Whitbeck, L. B., Conger, R. D., & Chyi-In, W. (1991). Intergenerational transmission of harsh parenting. *Developmental Psychology, 27,* 159–171.

Singer, J., Singer, D., & Rapaczynski, W. (1984). Family patterns and television viewing as predictors of children's beliefs and aggression. *Journal of Communication, 34*(2), 73–89.

Spearly, J. L., & Lauderdale, M. (1983). Community characteristics and ethnicity in the prediction of child maltreatment rates. *Child Abuse and Neglect, 7,* 91–105.

Spinetta, J. J., & Rigler, D. (1972). The child-abusing parent: A psychological review. *Psychological Bulletin, 77,* 296–304.

Sroufe, L. A. (1979). Emotional development. In J. Osofsky (Ed.), *Handbook of infant development* (pp. 462–516). New York: John Wiley & Sons.

Sroufe, L. A., Jacobvitz, D., Mangelsdorf, S., DeAngelo, E., & Ward, M. J. (1985). Generational boundary dissolution between mothers and their preschool children: A relationship systems approach. *Child Development, 56,* 317–325.

Sroufe, L. A., & Rutter, M. (1984). The domain of developmental psychopathology. *Child Development, 55,* 1184–1199.

Stack, C. (1974). *All our kin: Strategies for survival in a black community.* New York: Harper & Row.

Starr, R. H., Jr. (1988). Physical abuse of children. In V. Van Hasselt, R. Morrison, A. Bellack, & M. Hersen (Eds.), *Handbook of family violence* (pp. 119–155). New York: Plenum.

Staub, E. (1971a). A child in distress: The influence of nurturance and modelling on children's attempts to help. *Developmental Psychology, 5,* 124–132.

Staub, E. (1971b). Use of role playing and induction in training for prosocial behavior. *Child Development, 42,* 805–816.

Staub, E. (1975a). *The development of prosocial behavior in children.* Morristown, NJ: General Learning Press.

Staub, E. (1975b). To rear a prosocial child: Reasoning, learning by doing, and learning by teaching others. In D. DePalma & J. Foley (Eds.), *Moral development: Current theory and research* (pp. 113–135). Hillsdale, NJ: Erlbaum.

Steele, B. F., & Pollock, C. (1968). A psychiatric study of parents who abuse infants and small children. In R. E. Helfer & C. H. Kempe (Eds.), *The battered child* (pp. 103–147). Chicago: University of Chicago Press.

Stehno, S. M. (1982). Differential treatment of minority children in service systems. *Social Work, 27*(1), 39–46.

Steinberg, L., Catalano, R., & Dooley, D. (1981). Economic antecedents of child abuse and neglect. *Child Development, 52,* 975–985.

Steiner, G. Y. (1981). *The futility of family policy.* Washington, DC: Brookings Institute.

Straus, M. (1983). Ordinary violence, child abuse, and wife-beating: What do they have in common? In D. Finkelhor, R. Gelles, G. Hotaling, & M. Straus (Eds.), *The dark side of families: Current family violence research* (pp. 213–234). Beverly Hills, CA: Sage.

Thompson, R. A., & Jacobs, J. E. (1991). Defining psychological maltreatment: Research and policy perspectives. *Development and Psychopathology, 3*(1), 93–102.

Trickett, P. K., Aber, J. A., Carlson, V., & Cicchetti, D. (1991). Relationship of socioeconomic status to the etiology and developmental sequelae of physical child abuse. *Developmental Psychology, 27*(1), 148–158.

Tronick, E. Z., Morelli, G. A., & Winn, S. (1987). Multiple caretaking of Efe (Pygmy) infants. *American Anthropologist, 89,* 96–106.

Tronick, E. Z., Ricks, M., & Cohn, J. (1982). Maternal and infant affective exchange: Patterns of adaptation. In T. Field & A. Fogel (Eds.), *Emotion and interaction: Normal and high-risk infants* (pp. 382–403). New York: Academic.

Turner, R., & Noh, S. (1983). Class and psychological vulnerability among women: The significance of social support and personal control. *Journal of Health and Social Behavior, 24,* 2–15.

U.S. Department of Labor, Office of Policy Planning and Research (1965). *The negro family: The case for national action.* Washington, DC: U.S. Government Printing Office.

Vasta, R. (1982). Physical child abuse: A dual-component analysis. *Developmental Review, 2,* 125–149.

Wallerstein, J. S. (1985). Changes in parent-child relationships during and after divorce. In E. Anthony & G. Pollock (Eds.), *Parental influences in health and disease* (pp. 317–348). Boston: Little, Brown.

Wallerstein, J. S., & Blakeslee, S. (1989). *Second Chances: Men, women and children a decade after divorce.* New York: Ticknor & Fields.

Watson, J. S. (1971). Cognitive perceptual development in infancy: Setting for the seventies. *Merrill-Palmer Quarterly, 17,* 139–152.

Weber, C. U., Foster, P. W., & Weikart, D. P. (1978). *An economic analysis of the Ypsilanti Perry Preschool Project.* Ypsilanti, MI: High/Scope.

Weinraub, M., & Wolf, B. (1983). Effects of stress and social supports on mother-child interactions in single- and two-parent families. *Child Development, 54,* 1297–1311.

Werner, E. E., & Smith, R. S. (1982). *Vulnerable but invincible: A longitudinal study of resilient children and youth.* New York: McGraw-Hill.

White, G. M., & Burnam, M. A. (1975). Socially cued altruism: Effects of modeling, instruction and age on public and private donations. *Child Development, 46,* 559–563.

Whiteman, M., Fanshel, D., & Grundy, J. F. (1987). Cognitive-behavioral interventions aimed at anger of parents at risk of child abuse. *Social Work, 32*(6), 469–476.

Wilson, H. (1974). Parenting in poverty. *British Journal of Social Work, 4,* 241–254.

Wilson, M. (1989). Child development in the context of the black extended family. *American Psychologist, 44,* 380–383.

Wise, S., & Grossman, T. (1980). Adolescent mothers and their infants: Psychological factors in early attachment and interaction. *American Journal of Orthopsychiatry, 50,* 454–467.

Wolfe, D. A. (1985). Child-abusive parents: An empirical review and analysis. *Psychological Bulletin, 97,* 462–482.

Woolley, P. V., & Evans, W. A., Jr. (1955). Significance of skeletal lesions in infants resembling those of traumatic origin. *Journal of the American Medical Association, 158,* 539–543.

Young, L. (1964). *Wednesday's children: A study of child neglect and abuse.* New York: McGraw-Hill.

Young, V. (1970). Family and childhood in a southern negro community. *American Anthropologist, 72,* 269–288.

Youngblade, L., & Belsky, J. (1989). Child maltreatment, infant-parent attachment security, and dysfunctional peer relationships in toddlerhood. *Topics in Early Childhood Education, 9,* 1–15.

Zabin, L., Astone, N., & Emerson, M. (1993). Do adolescents want babies? The relationship between attitude and behavior. *Journal of Research on Adolescence, 3*(1), 67–86.

Zigler, E., Taussig, C., & Black, K. (1992). Early childhood intervention: A promising preventative for juvenile delinquency. *American Psychologist, 47*(8), 997–1006.

Zuravin, S. J. (1988). Child maltreatment and teenage first births: A relationship mediated by chronic sociodemographic stress? *American Journal of Orthopsychiatry, 58,* 91–103.

Integrating Human Development Research with Policies and Programs Promoting the Life Chances of Youth: Developmental Contextualism and the Michigan State Institute for Children, Youth, and Families

Richard M. Lerner

Universities are in the knowledge business; what universities do is generate, transmit, preserve, and apply knowledge (Boyer, 1990). Increasingly over the course of the past decade, universities have been called upon to use these knowledge functions to address problems of community, business, and governmental bodies as these problems are defined by these stakeholders working collaboratively with universities. When such university-community collaboration occurs in regard to the knowledge functions of the university, outreach is occurring (Lerner, 1995; Provost's Committee on University Outreach, 1993). Thus, with impetus provided by funding agencies and foundations, by federal and state governments, by business and industry, and by members of the grassroots community, a cultural change has begun to occur in the role that institutions of higher learning play in contributing to the critical issues facing society (Boyer, 1990; Lynton & Elman, 1987).

These issues include persistent and pervasive poverty; problems of economic development, health care; environmental quality; and issues confronting children and families (school failure, crime, family and community violence, drug and alcohol use and abuse, and unsafe sex and teenage parenting). Given the press by stakeholders to engage such concerns, universities have been challenged to view their scholarship from a perspective that is issue-focused rather than disciplinarily based (Boyer, 1990; Lynton & Elman, 1987). That is, the problems facing America are not ones having bases or solutions that fall neatly into disciplinary categories (Schiamberg, 1985, 1988). As such, the challenge given to American universities—the "demand" evoking university culture change—is to bring integrative scholarship to bear on these problems (Brown, 1987).

This focus on stakeholder-defined problems impels universities to work more closely with the communities wherein these problems reside. Indeed, it is the creation of such community-collaborative scholarship that, today, is perhaps the core intellectual issue around which discussions of changes in the American university system reside (Lynton & Elman, 1987). At its most basic level, this issue involves a revitalization and recommitment to the integration and unity of knowledge, including a unity involving all the above-noted knowledge functions of the university (Boyer, 1990).

Such knowledge integration, especially when it is embedded in an attempt to integrate scholarship and outreach (or, in other words, to create outreach scholarship), is difficult to pursue within disciplinarily-oriented university units (e.g., departments of psychology, sociology, chemistry, or literature). The traditional reward system in American universities has been associated with being responsive to the presses of disciplines and with pursuing the rewards that such responsivity can facilitate (e.g., publications in peer-reviewed journals, grants approved through the peer review process, prestige in peer/ professional organizations, and favorable tenure and promotion decisions accorded to those obtaining supportive letters from distinguished peers from one's discipline). In turn, the traditional reward system has not been responsive to work aimed at meeting the needs/presses of communities (Boyer, 1994; Votruba, 1992).

As a consequence of the stance of the disciplines, and in recognition of the political, economic, and social pressures to respond to the needs and interests of community stakeholders, many universities—and arguably perhaps especially land-grant institutions (Lerner & Miller, 1993; Miller & Lerner, 1994)—have acted in one of two ways. Universities have either created institution-wide outreach programs (Provost's Committee on University Outreach, 1993) or developed outreach scholarship units given the mission to organize and enhance the university's outreach scholarship in regard to a specific domain of community issues (e.g., economic development, environmental quality, or children, youth, and families).

As America's premier land-grant university, Michigan State University is committed to weaving outreach throughout the fabric of the university (Provost's Committee on University Outreach, 1993) and, as a consequence, the university has pursued both strategies. The office of the Vice Provost for University Outreach was created in 1990 to provide a vision of, and leadership for, outreach within and across all academic units of the institution. Shortly thereafter, in 1991, and through a partnership with and the leadership of the College of Human Ecology, the Institute for Children, Youth, and Families (ICYF) was created. The institute was given the mandate to integrate, enhance, and innovatively promote—across nine colleges of the university (i.e., Human Ecology, Communications Arts and Sciences, Social Science, Education, Urban Affairs Programs, Human Medicine, Osteopathic Medicine, Nursing, and Agriculture and Natural Resources/MSU Extension)—outreach scholarship pertinent to the diverse children, youth, and families of Michigan, the nation, and the world.

Michigan State University's Vice Provost for University Outreach (James C. Votruba) and the Dean of the College of Human Ecology (Julia R. Miller) believed that faculty collaboration across these units could be used as a mechanism to address pressing social needs, *when* such disciplinary integration was effectively coupled with appropriate professional application activities and community collaboration. Such collaborations require an engaging intellectual rationale, ideally one that demonstrates empirically that it is feasible and productive to integratively approach community, professional, and scholarly issues about children and families.

A useful theoretical frame exists for such multi-disciplinary, multiprofessional, and community collaboration pertinent to children, youth, and families. For ICYF, this frame lies in a specific instance of the developmental systems (Ford & Lerner, 1992) perspective, that is, in the developmental contextual view of human development (Lerner, 1986, 1991).

The Role of Developmental Contextualism in Framing Outreach Scholarship Pertinent to Diverse Children, Youth, and Families

Developmental contextualism is a theory of human development associated with land-grant and state universities' colleges of home economics (or, as they are often now termed, colleges of human ecology, human development, human sciences, or family science). Within these institutions, an integrative multidisciplinary view of human development arose to frame theory, research, and application about the dynamic (bidirectional) and changing relations between individuals and their social and physical ecology (Baltes, 1983; Bronfenbrenner, 1979, in preparation; Lerner & Miller, 1993; Lerner et al., 1994; Miller & Lerner, 1994). Developmental contextualism is an instance of this developmental systems perspective (Ford & Lerner, 1992) and, as such, conceives of the basic process of human development as involving changes in the integrated, or "fused" (Tobach & Greenberg, 1984), relations between the developing person and the multiple levels of his or her changing context (Lerner, 1991).

More specifically, developmental contextualism stresses that reciprocal relations, or "dynamic" interactions, exist among variables from multiple levels of organization (e.g., biology, psychology, social groups, and culture) (Lerner & Spanier, 1978). These dynamic relations structure human behavior. In addition, this system of integrated (fused) levels of organization is itself embedded in, and dynamically interactive with, history (Tobach, 1981); this temporality provides a change component to the multiple, integrated levels comprising human life. In other words, within developmental contextualism a changing configuration of interrelations among multiple levels of organization constitutes the basis of human life—of behavior and development (Ford & Lerner, 1992).

Thus, developmental contextualism is a view of human development that integrates the changes individuals undergo across their life spans with the features of their social, institutional, cultural, and historical contexts. Such integration includes what Bronfenbrenner (1979) terms the macro-ecology; embedded within this level of influence lie social policies and the intervention programs derived from such initiatives. The integration of research with policies and programs lies at the heart of outreach scholarship, at least as it is framed by developmental contextualism (Lerner & Miller, 1993; Lerner et al., 1994; Miller & Lerner, 1994). That is, within the developmental contextual perspective, policies and programs constitute theoretically derived interventions into the life span, steps taken to test ideas about how to optimize the lives of individuals and families. The evaluation of such policies and programs provides information not only about the functioning of such interventions but, also about the theoretical ideas of person-context relations from which such interventions are (ideally) derived. In other words, when attempts are made to explain the diversity of changing person-context relations that occur in the actual ecology of the human life course, then the evaluation of new or existing policies or programs becomes a means of testing developmental contextual accounts of such change processes (Lerner et al., 1994; Lerner, Ostrom, & Freel, in press; Ostrom, Lerner, & Freel, 1994).

Moreover, such explanatory research may derive from descriptive research that documents the similarities in the development of diverse groups. Clearly, differences in developmental pathways may readily elicit a search for explanations of distinct histories of person-context relations. In turn, however, similarities in developmental pathways may also be underlain by distinct person-context relations. Thus, whenever attempts are made to explain the course of human development, as it actually occurs in its ecologically valid context, theoretically planned changes in the context—the policies and programs involved in research-based outreach—can be used to test models of the ways through which developmental trajectories become either similar or different.

In other words, as emphasized in developmental contextualism, the variation in settings within which people live means that studying development in a standard (for example, a "controlled") environment does not provide information pertinent to the actual (ecologically valid) developing relations between individually distinct—diverse—people and their specific contexts (for example, their particular families, schools, or communities). This point underscores the need to conduct research in real-world settings and highlights the ideas that: (1) policies and programs constitute natural experiments, that is, planned interventions for people and institutions; and (2) the evaluation of such activities provides information about the utility of such outreach endeavors and, as well, feedback about the utility of the developmental contextual model from which the policies and programs were derived.

Advancing Policy-Relevant Outreach Scholarship through the MSU Series on Children, Youth, and Families

From a developmental contextual perspective, the specification of the policy implications of developmental contextual-oriented research (i.e., of research about dynamic and changing person-context relations) and/or the analysis or evaluation of the impact of policies on person-context relations is a vital part of outreach scholarship. Indeed, such policy-relevant scholarship is—from the developmental contextual theoretical frame used at ICYF—a key means through which the institute synthesizes basic (explanatory) and applied (intervention) scientific activity in a seamless way (Lerner et al., 1994); in so doing, ICYF integrates research and outreach to improve understanding of and service to the diverse youth, families, and communities served by the institute.

Because of the importance of policy-relevant outreach scholarship to the mission of the institute, key programs of ICYF are aimed at promoting such work (see Miller & Lerner, 1994, for a discussion). The MSU Series on Children, Youth, and Families, of which the volume by Diana Baumrind, *Child Maltreatment and Optimal Caregiving in Social Contexts,* is the inaugural publication, is an excellent case in point. The MSU series seeks to enhance outreach scholarship through the publication of books advancing the integration of research, policy, and intervention program issues and/or professional issues pertinent to these issues. As the inaugural publication of the series, it is gratifying to note that Baumrind's volume stands as an exemplar of both types of integration.

Both in the chapters comprising Baumrind's presentation and in the commentaries provided by Jackson and Abrams, one can see that the integration of scholarship from multiple disciplines, and the integration of such scholarship with professional activities, is used to enhance research and professional issues pertinent to the individual, familial, and broader contextual bases—including policy actions and historical influences—of child maltreatment. These integrations weave policy analysis into the understanding of extant individual and contextual data sets pertinent to child maltreatment and, as well, use such analyses to point to:

1. Assets and limitations in current research approaches (e.g., see Baumrind's specification of the uses and problems associated with existing data analytic and measurement techniques involved in the study of developmental systems)
2. Omissions in the current knowledge base (e.g., see Jackson's discussion of gaps that can be identified in the current child development literature, lacunae that can especially be seen when one adopts a developmental systems perspective that attends in particular to recent historical changes in the African American family, changes precipitated by coercive discriminatory, and indeed often blatantly racist welfare policies)
3. The effects of social policies on the developmental experiences and life chances of specific groups of youth and families in our society (e.g., see Abrams' analysis of

how welfare policies have levied a "poverty penalty" against poor children and families of color)

Together, then, the work of Baumrind, Jackson, and Abrams exemplifies the scope and utility of a developmental systems frame (e.g., such as developmental contextualism) in pursuing policy-relevant outreach scholarship pertinent to a key issue affecting youth and their families: child maltreatment. Indeed, the quality of their scholarship underscores the potential use of the approach to outreach scholarship pertinent to children, youth, and families pursued at ICYF (and promoted through programs such as the MSU series).

Accordingly, I will use the occasion of the publication of the work of Baumrind and her colleagues as a reason and as a basis for pursuing here broader discussion of policy issues pertinent to America's youth. This discussion is appropriate and timely not only because it occurs in relation to the exemplary contributions made by Baumrind and her colleagues to policy-relevant outreach scholarship. This discussion is also predicated on the fact that today, in America, there is no general national youth policy. As such, using the scholarship of Baumrind, Jackson, and Abrams as an example of what might be gained from the use of a developmental systems approach to policy-relevant research and outreach, I will discuss, first, some of the ideas that might be included in a national youth policy informed by an appreciation of the dynamic, developing relations between youth and their contexts. Second, I will turn to a discussion of specific policy foci that may be derived from a developmental contextual perspective. Finally, I will return to issues involving the contemporary American university and its system of faculty rewards; here, I will discuss changes in academic policy that will have to occur if policy-relevant outreach scholarship is to be more often pursued and, as a consequence, if universities are to better align their knowledge functions with the needs and issues of our nation's communities.

Toward the Development of a National Youth Policy

Policies represent standards or rules for the conduct of individuals, organizations, and institutions. The policies we formulate and follow structure our actions and enunciate to others how they may expect us to function in regard to the substantive issues to which our policies pertain. Moreover, policies reflect what we value, what we believe, and what we think is in our best interests; policies indicate the things in which we are invested and about which we care.

Today, all too many Americans do not see the need for a comprehensive and integrated national policy pertinent to all of our nation's children. To the contrary, many Americans see youth problems as associated with other people's children. Their stereotyped image of the at-risk or poor child is of a minority youth living in the inner city. Yet the probability that an American child or adolescent will be poor—and thus experience the several "rotten outcomes" (Schorr, 1988) of poverty—does not differ in regard to whether that youth lives in an urban or a rural setting (Huston, 1992). Moreover, the incidence of risk behaviors among our nation's youth (Dryfoos, 1990, 1994) extends the problems of America's children and adolescents far beyond the bounds associated with the numbers of poor or minority children.

For these reasons alone there appears to be ample reason for the development of a national youth policy pertinent to all of America's children and adolescents. There are additional reasons. Just as we may be concerned with developing better policies for sustaining and/or enhancing American agricultural, industrial, manufacturing, and business interests, it would seem clear that we must not lose sight of the need to sustain the communities—and the people—involved in the production, distribution, and consumption of the products of our economy.

Still, we often neglect the fact that problems of rural and urban youth—problems that are similarly structured, similarly debilitating, and similarly destructive of America's human capital—diminish significantly our present and future ability to sustain and enhance our economic productivity. Clearly, then, both from the standpoint of the problems of children and adolescents, and from the perspective of enlightened self-interest within America's industrial, agricultural, business, and consumer communities, policies need to be directed to enhancing youth development and preventing the loss of human capital associated with the breadth and depth of the problems confronting our children and youth.

Despite the historically unprecedented growth in the magnitude of the problems of America's youth, and of the contextual conditions that exacerbate these problems (e.g., changes in family structure and function, and in child and adolescent poverty rates), there have been few major policy initiatives taken to address these increasingly more direly changing circumstances. Indeed, as Hamburg (1992, p. 13) has noted,

> During the past three decades, as all these remarkable changes increasingly jeopardized healthy child development, the nation took little notice. One arcane but important manifestation of this neglect was the low research priority and inadequate science policy for this field. As a result, the nature of this new generation of problems was poorly understood; emerging trends were insufficiently recognized; and authority tended to substitute for evidence, and ideology for analysis. Until the past few years, political, business, and professional leaders had very little to say about the problems of children and youth. Presidents have tended to pass the responsibility to the states and the private sector. State leaders often passed the responsibility back to the federal government on the one hand or over to the cities on the other. And so it goes.

As a result of this "treatment" of social policy, the United States has no national youth policy per se (Hahn, 1994). Rather, policies, and the programs associated with them, tend to be focused on the family (e.g., Aid for Dependent Children, AFDC) and not on youth per se (Huston, 1992). As such, while these policies may influence the financial status of the family, they may not readily impact on, and certainly they fail to emphasize, youth development. That is, these policies do not focus on the enhancement of the capacities and the potentials of America's children and adolescents. For instance, a policy or program that provides a job for an unemployed single mother, but results in the placement of her child in an inadequate day care environment for extended periods of time, may enhance the financial resources of the family; yet it may do so at the cost of placing the child in an unstimulating and, possibly, detrimental environment.

Accordingly, if we are to substantially reduce the current waste of human life and potential caused by the problems confronting contemporary American youth, new policy options must be pursued, ones that focus on children and adolescents and that emphasize positive youth development and not only amelioration, remediation, and/or deterrence of problems. Thus, as recently argued by Pittman and Zeldin (1994, p. 53), "The reduction of problem behaviors among young people is a necessary policy goal. But it is not enough. We must be equally committed to articulating and nurturing those attributes that we wish adolescents to develop and demonstrate." Based on this perspective, Pittman and Zeldin (1994) forward several policy recommendations that, in combination, provide a means to develop a national youth policy supportive of the positive development of children and adolescents.

First, given their perspective, Pittman and Zeldin emphasize that policy must focus on youth development, not deterrence. Resources must be provided to ascertain the competencies and potentials of youth and to develop and evaluate programs designed to promote these positive attributes.

The support of research about, and programs for, positive youth development leads to a second policy recommendation forwarded by Pittman and Zeldin, one acknowledging the crucial role played by youth-serving organizations in enhancing the life chances of youth (cf. Carnegie Corporation, 1992; Dryfoos, 1990; National Research Council, 1993; Schorr, 1988). That is, policies must promote the financial support, and broad acceptance, of community-based youth organizations; such acceptance involves support of the socialization experiences and youth services provided by these organizations.

To promote the acceptance of community programs another policy step must be taken: "The policy goal of facilitating youth development must be translated and incorporated into the public institutions of education, employment and training, juvenile justice, and health services" (Pittman & Zeldin, 1994, p. 53). The translation involved in this policy step is predicated on the view that the promotion of youth development is not the exclusive provence of any single organization or agency, a view emphasized by Dryfoos (1990), Schorr (1988), and Hamburg (1992). To the contrary, then, an integrated, community-wide effort is necessary to foster positive youth development (Dryfoos, 1990; Hamburg, 1992; Schorr, 1988). Hamburg (1992) makes a similar point. He suggests three policy initiatives that, together, would enhance the capacity of communities to provide comprehensive and integrated services that promote positive youth development through the provision of effective programs delivered by a well-trained staff. Thus, Hamburg (1992, p. 166) notes that he would

> First, use federal and state mechanisms to provide funding to local communities in ways that encourage the provision of coherent, comprehensive services. State and federal funding should provide incentives to encourage collaboration and should be adaptable to local circumstances.
>
> Second, provide training programs to equip professional staff and managers with the necessary skills. Such programs would include training for collaboration among professionals in health, mental health, education, and social services, and would instill a respectful, sensitive attitude toward working with clients, patients, parents, and students from different backgrounds.
>
> Three, use widespread evaluation to determine what intervention is useful for whom, how funds are being spent, and whether the services are altogether useful.

Thus, policy must move from a focus on just developing effective programs to also building cohesive and effective communities (National Research Council, 1993; Pittman & Zeldin, 1994). Indeed, a recent report by the National Research Council (1993) notes that building supportive communities for youth faced with the destruction of their life chances "will require a major commitment from federal and state governments and the private sector, including support for housing, transportation, economic development, and the social services required by poor and low-income residents" (p. 239).

Finally, Pittman and Zeldin (1994) emphasize that for youth development programs to attain sustained successes—across the span of individual lives and across multiple generations—issues of individual and economic diversity must be clearly and directly confronted. Specifically, poverty and racism must be a continued, core focus of social policy. We must continue to be vigilant about the pernicious sequelae of poverty among children and adolescents, about the vast overrepresentation of minority youth among the ranks of our nation's poor, and about the greater probability that minority youth will be involved in the several problem behaviors besetting their generation.

In sum, then, the policy recommendations forwarded by Pittman and Zeldin (1994), Hamburg (1992), and the National Research Council (1993) stress the importance of comprehensive and integrative actions, involving both proximal community participation and the contributions of broader segments of the public and private sectors; of community-based evaluations; of diversity; and of promoting positive development across the life span. As may be recognized from my above discussion, these ideas are consistent with those brought to the fore by a developmental contextual perspective.

Indeed, I have argued that, from the perspective of developmental contextualism, policies—and the programs that do (or should) derive from them—merge (or, better, synthesize) basic and applied research. That is, policies and programs represent the means through which ecologically valid interventions may be enacted; evaluation of these interventions provides information, then, both about the adequacy of these "applied" endeavors and about "basic" theoretical issues of human development—about bases for the enhancement of the life courses of individuals, families, and communities (Lerner & Miller, 1993; Lerner et al., 1994).

Thus, from the perspective of developmental contextualism, policies, and the evaluation of their influences or outcomes, are actions that allow outreach scholars to make contributions to the understanding of, and to service to, the diverse children, adolescents, and families of our nation. Yet developmental contextualism provides more than a structure for the integration of basic and applied scholarship; it offers more than a frame for viewing policy engagement and programming as the "methods" for this integration, for the enactment of applied developmental science (Fisher & Lerner, 1994). In addition, there are several substantive directions for the development of policies pertinent to the youth of America that are promoted by developmental contextualism.

Implications of Developmental Contextualism for Youth Policy

There are at least six substantive foci of youth policy that may be derived from a developmental contextual perspective. The first is associated with the fact that developmental contextualism promotes an emphasis on the developmental system (Ford & Lerner, 1992). Within this system, development involves changes in relations between the growing person and his or her context (Lerner, 1991). Accordingly, to enhance development, to promote positive youth development, we must focus our efforts on this system, and not on either the individual (cf. Dryfoos, 1990; Schorr, 1988) or the context per se. As such, policies should be aimed at building programs that enhance relationships for youth across the breadth of the system, that is, with family members, peers, schools, and indeed across institutions of the proximal community and the more distal society.

Second, we must recognize that the system within which both youth and the programs aimed at them are embedded is also the system that contains the institutions that do (or could) provide resources for the promotion of youth and program development. Accordingly, we should use the multiple connections within the developmental system to create innovative approaches to generating resources to design, deliver, evaluate, and sustain effective youth-serving programs.

An example of the potential of such innovation is provided by Little (1993). He notes that all too often programs that might have a chance of being effective are not implemented or sustained. Little believes that one of the key reasons for this situation is that the procedure that has been used to secure program funding is not effective. That is, Little notes that whereas people with ideas start programs, often at a grassroots level, they typically have to go to a person with institutional power (e.g., a supervisor or a director/president of an organization) to find a potential advocate for the idea of the program. In turn, if this person with institutional power is persuaded to be an advocate for the program, he or she would (because of their role) be in a position to approach yet another person, someone with authority over resources (e.g., a program officer of a community foundation), to secure resources for the program. This procedure is, at best, only intermittently successful and, as such, Little believes it represents a weak link in the system through which program funding occurs. Accordingly, Little recommends that new linkages be formed in the system, ones between people of influence (i.e., those with control over resources) and people of ideas.

For instance, the International Youth Foundation promotes direct involvement of program officers from indigenous, grant-making, community foundations with the communities and the programs that they fund (Little, 1993). This "systems change" represents an important paradigm shift in the nature of the process involved in funding community-based youth programs.

A third policy implication for youth programs that is associated with developmental contextualism also is derived from an understanding of the developmental system within which young people are embedded: A system that is open to change for the better is also open to change for the worse. Accordingly, to effect sustained enhancement of the lives of youth, we need policies that promote long-term interventions. A one-shot intervention will not "inoculate" a youth for life against the potentially risk-actualizing perturbations of the developmental system within which he or she continues to live. Thus, we need to build (and fund) long-term—that is, life-span-oriented—"convoys" of social support (Kahn & Antonucci, 1980) to reinforce and further the positive developments that may accrue from effective youth programs.

The life-span nature of the developmental system within which youth are embedded is associated with a fourth implication for the development of policy. Transitions occur across the life span (Lerner & Spanier, 1980) and, often, these changes are qualitative in nature.

For example, the transitions involved in the period between childhood and early adolescence involve qualitative alterations in thinking abilities (i.e., "formal operational" ability emerges; Piaget, 1950, 1972); in emotions and personality (e.g., involving the psychosocial crisis of identity versus role confusions; Erikson, 1959); in social relationships (e.g., a shift in primary social group—from parents to peers—occurs; Guerney & Arthur, 1984); and in physiology (i.e., a new—sexual—drive and new hormones emerge during this period; A. Freud, 1969; Katchadourian, 1977). Given such qualitative changes, a program that provides a "goodness of fit" (Lerner & Lerner, 1989; Thomas & Chess, 1977) with the characteristics of the person during childhood may not continue to fit during adolescence. Accordingly, to be sure that the features of our programs remain qualitatively valid across the life span, we must monitor and calibrate our programs in order to attend to developmental changes and, as well, to contextual transitions (for example, involving the shift from elementary schools to middle or junior high schools; Simmons & Blyth, 1987).

A fifth policy implication, closely related to the idea of transitions across life, pertains to the issue of individual differences (diversity) and of transformations of individuals and contexts. Developmental contextualism stresses that diversity— of individuals, of contexts (including cultural ones), and of individual-context relations—is the "rule" of human behavior and development. "One size," that is, one type of intervention, "does not fit all." Policies and programs that are fit and effective for youth of one social, racial, ethnic, community, or cultural group may be irrelevant, poorly suited, or even damaging to youth with other characteristics of individuality. As such, policies and programs must be sensitive to, and organized to provide a goodness of fit with, the instances of human diversity relevant to the community or group to which they are directed.

Yet it will not be sufficient to just have policies that promote the development of diversity-sensitive programs. Such policies must promote as well a continuing awareness that individual differences increase as people develop across their life spans (Baltes, 1987; Schaie, 1979); as such, we must enable programs to be adjusted to fit the transformations in the character of individuality that emerge across life.

For instance, each human, as he or she develops across life, becomes increasingly different from other people as a consequence of his or her individual history of experiences, roles, and relationships (Lerner, 1988; Lerner & Tubman, 1989). Thus, initial characteristics of individuality are continually transformed over the course of life into different instances of individuality. As a consequence of such transformations in individuality, we must develop programs that are attentive to both initial and to emergent characteristics of individuality—of the person, of the context and, especially, of person-context relations.

The stress on individuality within developmental contextualism leads to a final implication for youth policy, one that returns us to the point that the outreach scholarship promoted by this perspective involves a merger of both basic and applied science. Developmental contextualism conceives of evaluation as providing information about policy and program efficacy and about how the course of human development can be enhanced through policies and programs. Indeed, because the development-in-context evaluation (DICE) procedures promoted by developmental contextualism (Lerner, 1995; Lerner et al., in press; Ostrom et al., 1994) involve the active participation of the individuals served by the program (Weiss & Greene, 1992), evaluation is also a means of empowering program participants and enhancing their capacities to engage in actions (i.e., program design, delivery, and evaluation) that promote their own positive development.

Accordingly, policies should promote the use of participatory-normative evaluation procedures (Weiss & Greene, 1992), such as those associated with the DICE model. Such evaluations will increase understanding of the lives developing within the context of the policies and programs one is implementing and, simultaneously, will inculcate greater capacities, and thus further empower, the youth, families, and communities involved in the programs that are being evaluated.

The important role that participatory evaluation procedures can play within a developmental contextual approach to
youth policy raises, once again, the issue of the potential
contributions of academe and of academicians to addressing the
problems besetting America's youth. If our nation's universities
are to be part of effective community coalitions enacting, and
fostering the continued development of, an integrative and
comprehensive national youth policy addressing the needs of
America's youth, social policy innovations must be coupled with
alterations in academic policies and practices. Without such
changes in the academy, our nation's universities will not be able
to be integral participants in addressing the needs of our
country's children and adolescents.

Dimensions of Academic Policy Change

American universities cannot become effective parts of the
solution to the problems besetting our nation's youth until
increased numbers of research and extension colleagues begin
to work collaboratively, both among themselves and with
the communities they serve. To bring researchers into this
collaboration will not only require university cultural change. In
addition, and arguably primarily, the reward systems of
American universities will have to be altered (Boyer, 1990, 1994;
Lerner et al., 1994; Votruba, 1992). Incentives will need to be
created that provide an exciting and attractive basis for the
reorientation of the work of established scholars and for the
reward of a career in outreach scholarship among junior faculty.
In addition, educators in each of the disciplines involved in the
study of human development should be presented with a vision
for beginning to train their students differently (Birkel, Lerner, &
Smyer, 1989; Fisher et al., 1993). An appreciation of systematic
change, context, and human relationships should be the
cornerstone of future graduate education.

These emphases are central points stressed in the growing
attention being paid among scholarly societies and universities
to the importance of training in applied developmental science
for future scholars and professionals in fields associated with

human development and education (Fisher & Lerner, 1994; Fisher et al., 1993). We should instill in these future scholars and professionals a greater appreciation of the importance of interindividual differences in the timing of causal, dynamic interactions—for the development of human diversity and for the contextual variation that is both a product and a producer of it (Lerner, 1982; Lerner & Busch-Rossnagel, 1981).

Furthermore, it is crucial that university merit, tenure, and promotion committees evaluating scientists studying development be urged to begin to consider the relative value of multidisciplinary collaborative, and hence multiauthored, publications, in comparison to within-discipline, single-authored products. Academic policy discussion must also involve the nature of the reception given by university review committees to the sort of contextual and collaborative research associated with developmental systems approaches to outreach scholarship. The issue to be debated here is whether we can train future cohorts of applied developmental scientists to engage productively in the multidisciplinary, multiprofessional, and community collaborations requisite for advancing understanding of the basic process of development and then not reward and value them (e.g., tenure and promote them) for successfully doing so.

If we follow a developmental contextual perspective that leads to the synthesis of science and outreach, then it would seem that we must devise means to assign value to, and reward, an array of collaborative, multidisciplinary, and multiprofessional activities (Votruba, 1992). Similarly, if we are to take seriously the need for change-oriented (and hence longitudinal), multilevel (and hence multivariate), and multidisciplinary research, we must recognize the need to educate government agencies and private foundations about the time and financial resources that should be given to such collaborative activities (McLoyd, 1994).

Simply, American universities must do more than provide a model for the integration of multiple academic disciplines and multiple professional activities with the community. They must embrace fully—by rewarding behavior consistent with—the ideal of multidimensional excellence, that is, of high-quality contributions across the breadth of the academic missions of research, teaching, and outreach. In other words, if universities are to significantly advance the integration of science and outreach for the diverse children, adolescents, and families of America's communities, sustained efforts must be made to build and maintain—through a revised academic reward system—a new, community-collaborative scholarly agenda.

This is the key challenge facing American universities as our nation approaches the next millennium (Boyer, 1994). And this is the path upon which we—as scholars, educators, youth-serving professionals, volunteers, and, most basically, citizens— must embark. Indeed, the stakes are high, not only for universities but, more important, for an American society faced with the loss of much of the human capital represented by its children and adolescents.

Conclusions

Ultimately, we must all continue to educate ourselves about the best means available to promote enhanced life chances among *all* of our youth, but especially those whose potentials for positive contributions to our nation are most in danger of being wasted (Lerner, 1993). The collaborative expertise of the research, policymaking, and intervention programming communities can provide much of this information, especially if it is obtained in partnership with strong, empowered communities. Policies promoting such coalitions will be an integral component of a national youth development policy aimed at creating caring communities having the capacity to nurture the healthy development of our children and youth.

There is no time to lose in the development of such policies. America as we know it—and, even more, as we believe it can be—will be lost unless we act now. All the strengths and assets of our universities, all of our institutions, and all of our people must be marshalled for this effort.

The agenda is clear and the means to achieve it appear available. We need only the will. And this motivation will be able to be readily evoked when Americans recognize the validity of the point made by Marian Wright Edelman (1992), President of the Children's Defense Fund, that "In the waning years of the twentieth century, doing what is right for children and doing what is necessary to save our national economic skin have converged." Let us work together to save our children, to save our families and communities, and—superordinately—to save America.

REFERENCES

Baltes, P. B. (1983). Life-span developmental psychology: Observations on history and theory revisited. In R. M. Lerner (Ed.), *Developmental psychology: Historical and philosophical perspectives* (pp. 79–111). Hillsdale, NJ: Erlbaum.

Baltes, P. B. (1987). Theoretical propositions of life-span developmental psychology: On the dynamics between growth and decline. *Developmental Psychology, 23,* 611–626.

Birkel, R., Lerner, R. M., & Smyer, M. A. (1989). Applied developmental psychology as an implementation of a life-span view of human development. *Journal of Applied Developmental Psychology, 10,* 425–445.

Boyer, E. L. (1990). *Scholarship reconsidered: Priorities of the professoriate.* Princeton, NJ: The Carnegie Foundation for the Advancement of Teaching.

Boyer, E. L. (1994, March 9). Creating the new American college [Point of View column]. *The Chronicle of Higher Education* (p. A48).

Bronfenbrenner, U. (1979). *The ecology of human development.* Cambridge, MA: Harvard University Press.

Bronfenbrenner, U. (In preparation). The ecology of developmental processes. In R. M. Lerner (Ed.), *Theoretical models of human development.* Volume 1 of the *Handbook of Child Psychology* (5th ed.), Editor-in-Chief: William Damon. New York: John Wiley & Sons.

Brown, N. A. (1987). *Youth development in the land-grant university.* McDowell lecture delivered at the Pennsylvania State University, University Park, PA.

Carnegie Corporation of New York. (1992). *A matter of time: Risk and opportunity in the nonschool hours.* Available from Carnegie Council on Adolescent Development, P.O. Box 753, Waldorf, MD 20604.

Dryfoos, J. G. (1990). *Adolescents at risk: Prevalence and prevention.* New York: Oxford University Press.

Dryfoos, J. G. (1994). *Full service schools: A revolution in health and social services of children, youth and families.* San Francisco: Jossey-Bass.

Edelman, M. W. (1992). *The measure of our success: A letter to my children and yours.* Boston: Beacon Press.

Erikson, E. H. (1959). Identity and the life-cycle. *Psychological Issues, 1,* 18–164.

Fisher, C. B., & Lerner, R. M. (Eds.). (1994). *Applied developmental psychology.* New York: McGraw-Hill.

Fisher, C. B., Murray, J. P., Dill, J. R., Hagen, J. W., Hogan, M. J., Lerner, R. M., Rebok, G. W., Sigel, I., Sostek, A. M., Smyer, M. A., Spencer, M. B., & Wilcox, B. (1993). The national conference on graduate education in the applications of developmental science across the life span. *Journal of Applied Developmental Psychology, 14,* 1–10.

Ford, D. L., & Lerner, R. M. (1992). *Developmental systems theory: An integrative approach.* Newbury Park, CA: Sage.

Freud, A. (1969). Adolescence as a developmental disturbance. In G. Caplan & S. Lebovier (Eds.), *Adolescence* (pp. 5–10). New York: Basic Books.

Guerney, L., & Arthur, J. (1984). Adolescent social relationships. In R. M. Lerner & N. L. Galambos (Eds.), *Experiencing adolescents: A sourcebook for parents, teachers, and teens* (pp. 87–118). New York: Garland.

Hahn, A. B. (1994). Towards a national youth development policy for young African-American males: The choices policymakers face. In R. B. Mincy (Ed.), *Nurturing young black males: Challenges to agencies, programs, and social policy* (pp. 165–186). Washington, DC: The Urban Institute Press.

Hamburg, D. A. (1992). *Today's children: Creating a future for a generation in crisis.* New York: Time Books.

Huston, A. C. (Ed.) (1992). *Children in poverty: Child development and public policy.* Cambridge: Cambridge University Press.

Kahn, R. L., & Antonucci, T. C. (1980). Convoys over the life course: Attachment, roles, and social support. In P. B. Baltes & O. G.

Brim (Eds.), *Life-span development and behavior, 3* (pp. 253–286). Hillsdale, NJ: Erlbaum.

Katchadourian, H. (1977). *The biology of adolescence.* San Francisco: Freeman.

Lerner, R. M. (1982). Children and adolescents as producers of their own development. *Developmental Review, 2,* 342–370.

Lerner, R. M. (1986). *Concepts and theories of human development* (2nd ed.) New York: Random House.

Lerner, R. M. (1988). Personality development: A life-span perspective. In E. M. Hetherington, R. M. Lerner, & M. Perlmutter (Eds.), *Child development in life-span perspective* (pp. 21–46). Hillsdale, NJ: Erlbaum.

Lerner, R. M. (1991). Changing organism-context relations as the basic process of development: A developmental-contextual perspective. *Developmental Psychology, 27,* 27–32.

Lerner, R. M. (1993). Early adolescence: Towards an agenda for the integration of research, policy, and intervention. In R. M. Lerner (Ed.), *Early adolescence: Perspectives on research, policy, and intervention* (pp. 1–13). Hillsdale, NJ: Erlbaum.

Lerner, R. M. (1995). *America's youth in crisis: Challenges and options for programs and policies.* Thousand Oaks, CA: Sage.

Lerner, R. M., & Busch-Rossnagel, N. (1981). Individuals as producers of their development: Conceptual and empirical bases. In R. M. Lerner & N. A. Busch-Rossnagel (Eds.), *Individuals as producers of their development: A life-span perspective* (pp. 1–36). New York: Academic.

Lerner, R. M., & Lerner, J. V. (1989). Organismic and social contextual bases of development: The sample case of early adolescence. In W. Damon (Ed.), *Child development today and tomorrow* (pp. 69–85). San Francisco: Jossey-Bass.

Lerner, R. M., & Miller, J. R. (1993). Integrating human development research and intervention for America's children: The Michigan State University model. *Journal of Applied Developmental Psychology, 14,* 347–364.

Lerner, R. M., Miller, J. R., Knott, J. H., Corey, K. E., Bynum, T. S., Hoopfer, L. C., McKinney, M. H., Abrams, L. A., Hula, R. C., & Terry, P. A. (1994). Integrating scholarship and outreach in human development research, policy, and service: A developmental contextual perspective. In D. L. Featherman, R. M. Lerner,

& M. Perlmutter (Eds.), *Life-span development and behavior, 12* (pp. 249–273). Hillsdale, NJ: Erlbaum.

Lerner, R. M., Ostrom, C. W., & Freel, M. A. (In press). Preventing health compromising behaviors among youth and promoting their positive development: A developmental-contextual perspective. In J. Schulenberg, J. L. Maggs, & K. Hurrelmann (Eds.), *Health risks and developmental transitions during adolescence.* New York: Cambridge University Press.

Lerner, R. M., & Spanier, G. B. (Eds.). (1978). *Child influences on marital and family interaction: A life-span perspective.* New York: Academic.

Lerner, R. M., & Spanier, G. B. (1980). *Adolescent development: A life-span perspective.* New York: McGraw-Hill.

Lerner, R. M., & Tubman, J. (1989). Conceptual issues in studying continuity and discontinuity in personality development across life. *Journal of Personality, 57,* 343–373.

Little, R. R. (1993, March). *What's working for today's youth: The issues, the programs, and the learnings.* Paper presented at an ICYF Fellows Colloquium, Michigan State University, East Lansing.

Lynton, E. A., & Elman, S. E. (1987). *New priorities for the university: Meeting society's needs for applied knowledge and competent individuals.* San Francisco: Jossey-Bass.

McLoyd, V. C. (1994). Research in the service of poor and ethnic/racial minority children: A moral imperative. *Family and Consumer Sciences Research Journal, 23,* 56–66.

Miller, J. R., & Lerner, R. M. (1994). Integrating research and outreach: Developmental contextualism and the human ecological perspective. *Home Economics Forum, 7,* 21–28.

National Research Council. (1993). *Losing generations: Adolescents in high-risk settings.* Washington, DC: National Academy Press.

Ostrom, C. W., Lerner, R. M., & Freel, M. A. (1994). Building the capacity of youth and families through university-community collaborations: The development-in-context evaluation (DICE) model. Available from the Institute for Children, Youth, and Families, Michigan State University, Suite 27 Kellogg Center, East Lansing, MI 48824.

Piaget, J. (1950). *The psychology of intelligence.* New York: Harcourt Brace.

Piaget, J. (1972). Intellectual evolution from adolescence to adulthood. *Human Development, 15,* 1–12.

Pittman, K. J., & Zeldin, S. (1994). From deterrence to development: Shifting the focus of youth programs for African-American males. In R. B. Mincy (Ed.), *Nurturing young black males: Challenges to agencies, programs, and social policy* (pp. 45–55). Washington, DC: The Urban Institute Press.

Provost's Committee on University Outreach. (1993). *University outreach at Michigan State University: Extending knowledge to serve society: A report by the Provost's Committee on University Outreach.* Michigan State University.

Schaie, K. W. (1979). The primary mental abilities in adulthood: An exploration in the development of psychometric intelligence. In P. B. Baltes & O. G. Brim Jr. (Eds.), *Life-span development and behavior, 2* (pp. 67–115). New York: Academic.

Schiamberg, L. B. (1985). *Child and adolescent development.* New York: Macmillan.

Schiamberg, L. B. (1988). *Child and adolescent development* (2nd ed.). New York: Macmillan.

Schorr, L. B. (1988). *Within our reach: Breaking the cycle of disadvantage.* New York: Doubleday.

Simmons, R. G., & Blyth, D. A. (1987). *Moving into adolescence: The impact of pubertal change and school context.* Hawthorne, NJ: Aldine.

Thomas, A., & Chess, S. (1977). *Temperament and development.* New York: Brunner/Mazel.

Tobach, E. (1981). Evolutionary aspects of the activity of the organism and its development. In R. M. Lerner & N. A. Busch-Rossnagel (Eds.), *Individuals as producers of their development: A life-span perspective* (pp. 37–68). New York: Academic.

Tobach, E., & Greenberg, G. (1984). The significance of T. C. Schneirla's contribution to the concept of levels of integration. In G. Greenberg & E. Tobach (Eds.), *Behavioral evolution and integrative levels* (pp. 1–7). Hillsdale, NJ: Erlbaum.

Votruba, J. C. (1992). Promoting the extension of knowledge in service to society. *Metropolitan Universities, 3* (3) 72–80.

Weiss, H. B., & Greene, J. C. (1992). An empowerment partnership for family support and education programs and evaluations. *Family Science Review, 5,* 131–148.

Contributors

Diana Baumrind is a research scientist at the Institute of Human Development at the University of California in Berkeley (UCB). She received her Doctor of Philosophy in clinical, developmental, and social psychology at UCB where for the last thirty years she has conducted her well-known longitudinal study, The Family Socialization and Developmental Competence Project. Dr. Baumrind is the leading authority on how contrasting patterns of parental authority affect the development of character and competence in children and adolescents. In addition to her seminal work on childrearing, Dr. Baumrind is known for her work on ethics and more recently on social policy applications of scholarly work on the family.

Jacquelyne Faye Jackson is a research scholar at the Institute of Human Development at UCB. She received her B.A. at Stanford, and her Master of Social Work and Doctor of Philosophy in developmental psychology at Berkeley. She has contributed several important journal articles on applicability to the African American context of research on attachment and behavioral genetics. Dr. Jackson is currently a co-principal investigator on a research project called Bridging Family, School and College, Contexts of Discovery: Origins of Competence in Minority Youth.

L. Annette Abrams has devoted her professional career to human services in the policy arena. She is Associate Director for Child, Youth and Family Policy in the Office of the Vice Provost for University Outreach at Michigan State University and an evaluation consultant for the W. K. Kellogg Foundation. Prior to her arrival at MSU in 1992 with a joint associate directorship for policy in the Institute for Children, Youth, and Families and the

Institute for Public Policy and Social Research, Abrams directed the Michigan Office of Children and Youth Services. She received her B.A. in politics and government from Howard University in 1968. Abrams has published and presented numerous papers on policy issues for scholarly journals and symposia, state and federal government committees, and the media.

Paul H. Mussen is Professor of Psychology Emeritus and former director of the Institute of Human Development at UCB. He is the author (with J. Conger, K. Kagan and A. Huston) of seven editions of *Child Development and Personality*, the author of *Roots of Prosocial Behavior in Children* (with N. Eisenberg), and editor of the *Handbook of Child Psychology*. He has served as president of the Western Psychological Association and Division 7 (Developmental) of the American Psychological Association.

Richard M. Lerner is a professor of family and child ecology, psychology, pediatrics and human development, and counseling, educational psychology, and special education. He is the Director of the Institute for Children, Youth, and Families at Michigan State University. A developmental psychologist, Lerner received a Ph.D. in 1971 from the City University of New York. He has been a fellow at the Center for Advanced Study in the Behavioral Sciences and is a fellow of the American Association for the Advancement of Science, the American Psychological Association, the American Psychological Society, and the American Association of Applied and Preventive Psychology. Lerner is the author or editor of 30 books and more than 200 scholarly articles and chapters. He is known for his theory of, and research about, relations between human development and contextual or ecological change. He is the founding editor of the *Journal of Research on Adolescence*.

Subject Index

Author Index

33.80